AGENDA

Exiles

AGENDA

CONTENTS

ESSAYS

Front cover: 'Interior' by Geraldine Wheeler who lives on the South Coast. See more of her work at www.geraldinewheeler.com .

Watercolour on back cover: 'Stone Cottage' by Johnny Marsh, artist and psychotherapist working with mental health charities in East Sussex.

This Exiles issue of *Agenda*
is dedicated to

Dennis O'Driscoll,

poet, essayist, ambassador
for poetry, and a charming,
supportive advisor to *Agenda*
for a decade.

Introduction

Welcome to this 'Exiles' issue of *Agenda* which has been brewing for quite some time.

I hope you will agree that these pages demonstrate the multiple ways a person can be an exile: not just by being ostracised or separated from your own country, but also by illness, death, by the feeling of being a loner, an outsider, even by being an 'exile' from the deepest or truest self in a person's psyche.

The translations/versions come from far and wide and are testimony to the power of poetry as a universally expressive and liberating force, cutting through boundaries, sects, creeds.

The two interviews – of Bernard O'Donoghue by William Bedford, and of Gezim Hajardi by Cristina Viti – analyse 'Exile' most articulately and profoundly in its multifarious aspects. I advise readers to peruse these sections first.

This issue is dedicated to Dennis O'Driscoll who served as an advisor to Agenda for many years and who suddenly and tragically died in December 2012. His regular phone calls and correspondence in his large, carefully formed handwriting gave heart when heart was almost lost in working, nay slaving, at this journal, with only two staff on board. His gentle encouragement and appreciation regularly fluffed up Agenda's feathers. It is wonderful to know that he had a funeral with full state honours, with an address by Seamus Heaney, whose biographer he was, who praised his poetry for moving Irish poetry out and away from its rural, small-farm imagery into the internet world of banks and text messaging and emails.

He was a dignified host, a noble diplomat for poetry and a very special spiritual man, loved by all who came across him.

This issue also has a very special start: with Jeremy Hooker's moving poem to Tony Conran, the memorable Welsh poet who also suddenly died around last Christmas, after coping heroically with cerebral palsy for most of his life. *Agenda* has honoured Tony in its pages and will continue to do so.

Don't forget to visit the website for further poems, paintings, Broadsheet 20, for reviews and more news; also for the Agenda online bookshop, and for the easy facility of subscribing online via Paypal.

Keep a watch on the website also for dates of launches and readings; also for when the submissions window will re-open.

Warm wishes to all our subscribers, readers and invisible supporters.

Patricia McCarthy

Jeremy Hooker

Poet among ferns

In memory of Tony Conran

i

Gift-giver,
what shall we give you?

What do you need
except to give – at home
in the reception of friends,
among compatriots?

ii

I think of you among ferns,
poet with a fernery –

plants of marginal places,
the tough, the delicate,

in crevices, in castle walls,
on mountain rock-fall,

ferns following streams
or deep in woodland –

a whole country of ferns
and you their poet.

iii

Maidenhair
Lady fern
Hart's-tongue
Spleenwort

Horsetails
of the coal deposits
Bracken with creeping rhizomes,
a life-history underground,
the air rich with spores –
ferns that have mastered the margins,
a whole country of ferns.

iv

Once, over head in bracken,
I found myself lost
yards from a country lane,
but lost, briefly in panic.
And what is one loss
but taste of the final loss –
poet with nothing to sell
but himself, some
poor notion of self,
alone and fearful of death?

v

Loneliness was the place
you came in from.

Out of the margins you came
to Wales and a home
on the March between languages.

And what you built there
became a place others could enter,
knowing ground underfoot,
the rich moulds, the life
of leaf-fall, the air
quick with spores:

a place for
'the whole body, the whole mind'.

vi

You know the way of the elegies:
mourning in the hall with black hearth,
lament of oak trees in the storm
that racks their limbs,
a tribe undone, bridge over the flood
smashed to matchstick.

These are not for you.
Rather a word of triumph,
a boast, if you like, a brag
of Conran the poet.

But if a brag, a quiet one,
a word befitting a poet walking away
on the path he has given us,
some word tough yet delicate,
true to a country of ferns.

Bernard O'Donoghue and William Bedford

Here Nor There

> 'In the real world, of course, there's no such person
> as a Bona-Fide traveller. They will pull
> the glass out of your hand and order you
> to go back to the place you came from,
> whatever you might have called that at the start.'
>
> 'Bona-Fide Travellers' by Bernard O'Donoghue

William Bedford: The idea of exile – or at least leaving home – is there from the start in your work. I'm thinking of a poem such as 'A Nun Takes the Veil' which you chose to open your first full collection *The Weakness* and eventually your *Selected Poems*. Could you take us 'back to the place' you yourself came from?

Bernard O'Donoghue: Well, I grew up in the north of County Cork, near a village called Cullen and a town called Millstreet. My father was a farmer there in the townland of Knockduff – at least he inherited the family farm there, but he hated farming. He worked as a travelling insurance salesman for the Sun Life of Canada, which meant he drove to picturesque places all over County Kerry mostly. In the summer we often travelled with him, for the trip. But he hated the selling too: he was the most unlikely salesman ever. My mother came from Manchester, from an Irish background. She did a History degree at Manchester University in a great era – people like Lewis Namier and A.J.P.Taylor taught her there. But she was an excellent farmer and did all the work around the place. Despite the Irish background and her principled fondness for Ireland and everything to do with it, she always seemed English, which made for a slight exoticism and anxiety about our place in the community – my two elder sisters and me. It was on the whole a very happy set-up I think. We went to Manchester for holidays, which was also exotic. We were Man City fans: my mother had been an enthusiastic attender at City and at Old Trafford for cricket in her youth; her father George McNulty sang in the Hallé choir – in fact they were pretty strange Manchester-Irish altogether. Her mother was Margaret Sheahan from Nohoval near Rathmore, four miles away from us. She went in for a kind of middle-class, aspirational style too – though she said she never felt at ease out of Ireland. I always think of her when I read Louis MacNeice saying 'I wish one could either *live* in Ireland or *feel oneself* in England.'

William Bedford: I think you left County Cork when you were sixteen? That's often an awkward age for most of us. Do you remember your feelings at leaving Ireland? And indeed arriving in England?

Bernard O'Donoghue: My father died suddenly at a football match in Cork (I was with him) in March 1962 when I was sixteen, yes. It was a huge shock of course: I remember a curious consequence of it – or I suppose it was that. I have never felt entirely at ease in the company of one other man since then: I feel more comfortable and safe with women (allowing for the other kinds of gender unease that arise there of course). I had already moved from the countryside to a school in Cork City that year, so in some ways that shift was a preparation for the move to Manchester. Idyllic as the country upbringing had been – and it really was in many ways: saving the hay, growing fond of the animals and so on – I loved both cities, Cork and Manchester. Leaving Ireland was strange, but we never wholly did: I have never not spent at least eight weeks in Ireland every year. And I loved Manchester (I still do): the bookshops and the sport – going to Maine Road, playing tennis in For Lane Park and so on. But above all the music: for the next ten years I was obsessed with classical music. I am not sure why: I think I saw it as the most certain route to self-improvement! I know nothing about the mechanics of music though: I still can't read music! But the experience that I *thought* I found most fulfilling was the Hallé at the Free Trade Hall, and chamber concerts and opera. I went every Saturday morning to Gibbs' second-hand record shop in Lower Moseley Street: it was Heaven. And of course the music scene there was quite a big deal: I saw the Oistrakhs and Rubinstein and Tortelier and Arrau – and of course Barbirolli all the time.

William Bedford: I remember you quoting Heaney saying 'strangers are people other than natives of County Derry'. Do you have any similar feelings, even after all these years, about County Cork?

Bernard O'Donoghue: I think I was paraphrasing Heaney's profound poem 'Broagh', about language and locality. I don't think I do feel like that about County Cork – though it is without question the place I love most and feel most at home in. But there are other places I am strongly attached to too: Manchester, as I have said, but by now of course Oxford where I have lived most of my life: forty-six years to be precise. My children have grown up here and they all live in the South-East of England. My wife (who is the classic 'more Irish than the Irish themselves' for which I am very grateful) is from the North-East of England. I discovered that area when I met Heather, and I was completely blown away by it: those wonderful shorelines and wild inland country around Teesside and Northumbria and North Yorkshire. The football results have three focuses of anxiety: Man City, Middlesbrough and Oxford United (where my son Tom is a season ticket-holder).

William Bedford: When did you begin writing? Was this just something you did naturally, an accepted part of your home and school life in Ireland, or a response to the changes when you moved to England?

Bernard O'Donoghue: No, I didn't do it naturally, or early. I was always keen on reading, especially Dickens and comic writing – like Lewis Carroll and *Three Men in A Boat*. But everything. When I moved to Cork City, the idea was that I would do Engineering at University College Cork. But I had an inspirational teacher of English and Irish at that school, Presentation College, Dan Donovan who is a great actor and theatre director (still flourishing in his nineties). His declamation of *Macbeth* won me over to English particularly. I remember one summer evening in 1962, reading 'The Ancient Mariner' in the flat I shared with my sisters on Donovan's Road: reading Orwell and Lawrence there as well. Then, when I moved to England and 'The Two Cultures', I had to choose one side or the other for A level, the Maths side (called 'the Moderns') or the literary side (called 'the Lits'). This was at the grammar school, St Bede's, where my grandfather went a hundred years back (I was very lucky they took me in there: why did they?). So I abandoned Maths with some reluctance. I was pretty good at it – at least I was very numerate, though I suspect I was conceptually pretty limited. I had another dabble with the positivist world when I worked with IBM for a year in 1968-9. I loved the people who worked in IBM, but I was useless at the work. But in my big reading days, I never aspired to write: it was a kind of dream, if that. Writing was an august thing that other people did: wonderful but out of my reach, except as a consumer. Like Music I suppose.

William Bedford: You went up to Lincoln College, Oxford, in 1965, and in a way, if we are going to be talking about forms of exile, this is a deepening of the 'differences', to pick up on one of the theorists' favourite words. You would have travelled not just from Irish English to English English, but in studying Old English and Middle English, gone back to the roots and the culture of the language. That was obviously the structure of the Oxford English degree, but can I ask you about the impact that literature had on you? I think you described 'The Seafarer' and 'The Wanderer' as your 'model for the perfectly formed lyric poem'?

Bernard O'Donoghue: Yes, that is right. Heaney said getting a letter from

13

the poetry editor of Faber was like hearing from God Almighty; I have to confess that my equivalent moment was the letter from the Senior Tutor at Lincoln, offering me a 'place to read English', on my birthday in 1964. It really was a kind of invitation to Heaven on earth. I loved medieval English (Chaucer especially), but in fact I did the general English course from *Beowulf* to 1900. If I had a specialising interest at that point it was Irish writing in English, rather than the medieval things: Yeats and Joyce and the Cork short story writers – especially Frank O'Connor. (I still think he deserves as high a place in world literature as Yeats and Joyce and Beckett and Heaney.) I enjoyed the English course immensely, but it didn't entirely match my enthusiasms – except maybe Chaucer and Shakespeare and Wordsworth and Dickens. Joyce was too modern for the course (Yeats got in because he had published 'a substantial body of work' by 1900). My friend and contemporary, Steven Rose, a brilliant son of Polish-Lithuanian refugees (his family history was horrifying though not much dwelt on: as a background it gave us all some sense of seriousness maybe), gave me both *Swann's Way* and *Ulysses*. There was a lot of heavy-duty reading outside the Oxford course, as well as in it of course; and – getting back to your question – there was a lot of 'other' in all that. I began loving the Anglo-Saxon elegies so much when I started teaching them in 1971. I have loved teaching Old English all my working life – though I never felt I had the total grasp of it that the real pros had. I still think that 'The Wanderer' and the others are my perfect model, mainly I think because of the way they balance a purported physical, sensory experience with a serious moral conclusion. They are consolations, both generically and in practice. They are also very brilliant in language and imagery of course – and mysterious. A good poem must always hold something in reserve. And it must, ultimately, be serious I think! That is what I admire so much about those poems.

William Bedford: I don't know whether I'm inventing a question here, but I'm wondering whether there was anything of C.S. Lewis's experience in your own experience. You remember what he wrote in *Surprised by Joy* about the Norse sagas and his own sense of 'northernness', something in that literature which called to something deep within himself. Obviously, if the call was really deep you might not even be aware of it, but were you conscious of anything like that?

Bernard O'Donoghue: That is very interesting. Lewis was Northern Irish Protestant, and very religious of course: I grew up as a very religious-observant Southern Irish Catholic, but I think in a less profound way (I am not as profound a thinker as Lewis). But there are affinities I think: I am sure the reason I took to the medieval academic world was that I half-knew it already, from the Catholic upbringing. You were familiar with doctrines like the Immaculate Conception and the Real Presence and the Infallibility of the Pope at the age of eight, so the apologetics that medievalism entailed was not such a big deal. More interestingly maybe, you encountered words like 'vouchsafe', 'intercession' and 'supplications' younger even than that, without any sense of what they meant. It was like learning a foreign language unsystematically – and at the same time I was learning Irish at school from the age of five. Both the philology and the uncomprehended language were coded in you from the start. So I did a two-year postgraduate degree in the Middle English period (1100-1500), and I took papers in Medieval Philosophy and in Dante. I nearly failed the B.Phil. because I did Dante without knowing Italian (testing to the utmost T.S. Eliot's theory that you can read Dante without a proper knowledge of Italian). I also never got the hang of Philosophy – Aquinas, Scotus and Ockham. Scotus was full of suggestive phrases – the things Hopkins liked (*haecceitas* and all that) – but my brain certainly wasn't strong enough to hold his sophistical arguments in an ordered sequence. *De Primo Principio* is the hardest book in the world. But I think, as I say, I was programmed to think that not understanding things did not matter: that there is even a suggestive miasma around the uncomprehended! Anyway, what took me into that suggestive nightmare was the dim half-grasp I had from serving Mass and gabbling Latin. '*Sursum corda*'. '*Habemus ad Dominum*'. I loved William of Ockham's logic though; it anticipated some of what goes on in French modern literary theory. He would be my nomination for the greatest Englishman, in response to that survey a few years ago. Ahead of Shakespeare and Churchill: even of Bruce Forsyth.

William Bedford: You completed your undergraduate and postgraduate studies in 1971, and 'after this, you might say, nothing else really happened'. You settled in Oxford with a lectureship at Magdalen College (1971-1995) and fellowship at Wadham College (1995-2011), and a career of teaching and writing. But Carpenter's point, of course, in talking of Tolkien, is that the ordinary life may not be the best guide to the secret life of the poems. You published three pamphlet collections before *The Weakness*. We've detailed these in the bibliography, but can you tell us something about the circumstances of those collections?

Bernard O'Donoghue: It all started with John Fuller who was my modern colleague at Magdalen College. I was extremely fortunate – again – to be given a lectureship in Medieval English there by Emrys Jones and John Fuller in 1971, straight after I had scraped through the B.Phil. John, who was already an acclaimed young poet, ran the college poetry society, the John Florio. You had to submit a poem anonymously to go to the meetings, so I did. It was the only way of meeting the students in a social and bibulous way, and it was great fun. John has a genius for encouraging and developing writers: he criticised the submitted poems with the same Empsonian rigour that he applied to everything in the English canon. Even more remarkable, he published the members' work – often fairly basic stuff – in small, beautifully bound pamphlets, on his Sycamore Press, on an ancient, oily machine in his garage. I have never encountered such wholly disinterested generosity anywhere else. Many people started in that way with John: James Fenton, David Harsent, Alan Hollinghurst, Mick Imlah.... So my first publication was a beautiful green pamphlet called *Razorblades and Pencils*, published by John in 1982 (when I was thirty-six: I was far from a precocious beginner). The second pamphlet, if that is the correct term, was *The Absent Signifier* in 1990, a beautiful, large, pale blue booklet, published by Peter Scupham at his Mandeville Press. This was another generous and disinterested enterprise, and again it was a huge boost. The other pre-*Weakness* book was of a different order though: *Poaching Rights*, published in Ireland by Peter Fallon at Gallery Press in 1987. This was my first full-scale slim volume: a really beautifully made book – dark red, and in hardback and paperback. That was a great breakthrough and I have an enduring attachment to it. I am deeply grateful to Peter Fallon who was a marvellous, alert editor.

William Bedford: How do you approach the writing of each poem? What is the writing process like for you?

Bernard O'Donoghue: It varies, doesn't it. Very occasionally the thing falls into place and it hardly requires any adjustment. Sometimes something gets requisitioned which is a great help. I tend to have scraps hanging around unmodified for years; mostly they don't come to anything, but just occasionally something sparks them back into life. That is the exception rather than the rule though. I sometimes think that I have boxed myself in to an extent that makes it almost impossible for me to write anything. Mostly I don't write in rhyme because I have this idea that the form somehow becomes the objective and can get in the way of the 'message' (though I know this is not true of – e.g. – Yeats or Larkin!). Then I suspect poems that are all message: poems that have a design on us, as Keats said, so that is another possibility closed off. I don't write comic poems: I don't like 'light verse', even when other people write it. I am afraid of all the things it is right to be afraid of: self-righteousness, preaching, humour. So what is left? What *do* I write about? I like David Constantine's notion of 'poems that matter'. But by the time I have finished setting up the constraints, there isn't much left *to* matter. I keep hearing myself saying to fretful writers 'you can't write too little'; but I think I may have overdone that principle. I don't write fiction: for whatever reason, I can't. But on the odd occasions when I have tried, I go through the same process. I hate surrealism: again, not *serious* enough. (Actually, I do like comic fiction though.) But then I don't like the obsessive current school of novel-writing that says you have to research all the details to make sure it is getting things right: what is the point of writing in fiction at all then? So there isn't much of a gap between those two positions. Medieval fictions are the best: *Troilus and Criseyde* or *Gawain and the Green Knight*. And *Piers Plowman* is nice and serious.

William Bedford: Is a critically sophisticated self-consciousness a problem for a writer? I'm thinking about the difference between Coleridge's synthetic and analytical imagination, the difference between writing and teaching poetry?

Bernard O'Donoghue: I think one of the things that excites you into writing is reading and wanting to – in a pale way – do likewise. I agree with what has become a bit of a mantra with creative writing teachers: if you want to write, you must read. I think my previous answer deals with this in a way, doesn't it. But I find I don't apply the same critical faculties to my own writing at all. I think maybe that is the problem with poetry like Empson's (he is my favourite critic): it is like writing in a mirror so that the critical evaluation comes first. I think maybe the real answer is I don't know, because I don't teach poetry much in that prac-crit, Empsonian way, much as I admire it. The kind of poetry I teach, or at least the way I teach it, tends to have a historical bias: 'Yeats in his context' or 'Chaucer in his time', kind of thing. I am no good at workshops for this reason, and I always say no to them now: the only thing I can find to say is 'That looks fine to me. I mean, do you *want* to write poetry?' I briefly coached a very good rowing eight and I had exactly the same feeling. I love the social side of teaching – its friendliness. But I am a hopeless teacher as far as telling people things they don't know goes, or pointing them in some other direction. Recently I have felt I am starting to get the idea – but sadly I have just retired.

William Bedford: In *Heaney and the Language of Poetry* you made a comment about the significance of form for Irish poets since the end of the nineteenth century: 'a consciousness of Irish poetic forms has been unignorable since the end of the last century for all Irish poets writing in English'. How important are such forms in your own practice?

Bernard O'Donoghue: Not very important: indeed I don't think that what I said there about forms is true. I am hoping to update that book to take account of Heaney's magnificent later work and the bearing of language on it; but if I do I will have to change some of those early propositions. Certainly, it is nonsense to say that those forms are 'unignorable' for '*all* Irish poets writing in English'. Sorry, everybody! On the other hand, there has to be some affinity between the writer's writing and their speaking voice and accent, at least in the kind of colloquial-tending poetic language I write in. That may be the real answer to your question about the 'writing process' above. Maybe that is the one way out I allow myself.

William Bedford: You published four full-length volumes between 1991 and 2003. Even allowing for the fact that several of the poems in *The Weakness* had already been published in pamphlet collections, this is a remarkable achievement. Shelley's 'inconstant wind' blows when it will, I know, but are you aware of any particular reason for this sudden increase in productivity?

Bernard O'Donoghue: Well, *The Weakness* in 1991 was a bit of a cheat because it drew on some poems that had been in *Poaching Rights* which I felt was an equally 'whole' book. The next three were fairly short I suppose; I always felt they were *just* reaching their target in size. I had a series of excellent but fairly permissive editors at Chatto who left things as I gave them. (Not that they weren't helpful: Rebecca Carter for instance took a strong line against the first title I proposed for *Outliving* – it was such a bad title that I can't bear to repeat it here! She was a terrific editor.) I don't think there was anything in my circumstances that made me write. 1995 was my fiftieth year and it was a bit of an *annus mirabilis*. It was the year I started at Wadham, it was a glorious summer when I cycled around Sligo during my first Yeats summer school there, and *Gunpowder* won the Whitbread Prize. The next two books came at four-year intervals. I liked the titles of both of them, and of course all those Chatto books had wonderful covers. Then there was a bit of a gap after 2003, interrupted by the *Selected Poems* in 2008.

William Bedford: *The Weakness* came out in 1991, and in a comment Tom Paulin talked of your gift for 'displacing our more predictable reactions to things as they are so that we glimpse their underlying tragedy'. The storyteller's narrative skill is apparent from the start. Is that a natural facility inherited from rural life and Irish literary traditions?

Bernard O'Donoghue: I am not sure that it is directly that. But it certainly links back to Frank O'Connor and the Cork short story, yes. A lot of my poems are kind of short stories *manqué* I think. Some of the better poems really are shrunken short stories – like 'The Fool in the Graveyard' and '*Ter Conatus*' I suppose. But there was still a lot of storytelling in the Irish countryside in the 1950s. Our neighbour Kate Mac (the woman in whose house we still spend the holidays) was a great teller of stories. But then she read *Tess* and English women's magazines about the Royal family. And one of the most successful acts on Irish radio in the 1950s were the stories told by the *seanchaí* (roughly meaning 'traditional storyteller'), the great actor Eamon Kelly. His stories were a wonderful mixture of wit and the everyday and the medieval surreal. So there was a lot of it about, yes. It was reinforced by medieval literature again: I love the title of A.B. Lord's book about local storytelling and epic, *The Singer of Tales*.

William Bedford: There's a rich variety of linguistic registers in these poems, and the storytelling is obviously aided by the vernacular – 'I stopped the once' and 'You have the Irish well' for instance. Are these conscious literary choices, or do you still hear the rhythms and idioms of rural speech as you write?

Bernard O'Donoghue: Sometimes I hear them, yes. I worry that they can be a bit mannered, though. They are accurate enough reproductions I think – but they have to be used sparingly. 'You have the Irish well', is a kind of parodic version of what native Irish speakers traditionally said to compliment the schoolchildren who were packed off to the *gaeltacht* for the summer holidays. It is beautifully evoked in Heaney's prose-poem 'The Stations of the West'. It was said that the visiting children were called the '*lá breá*'s – 'fine days' – because that was the extent of their Irish. I do find the survival of nonstandard expressions in colloquial usage very tempting.

William Bedford: There is a good deal of cruelty in the rural life explored in *The Weakness*: the black humour of 'O'Regan the Amateur Anatomist', the viciousness of hare coursing in 'The Saga of McGuinness's Dog'. But these are deeply humane poems 'Ashamed of the binocular intrusion,/Like breath on eggs or love pressed too far'. Is there any sense of personal catharsis in work such as this?

Bernard O'Donoghue: Yes, I think so – or a kind of collective, social catharsis. Country life is extremely brutal. There is an (English) joke, about the sheepdog-trainer on *One Man and his Dog*, who is asked to what he attributes his extraordinary success in training the dogs? He replies 'It's simple really. It just takes a little bit of kindness – and a lot of cruelty.' That is particularly what children growing up in the country witness. Indeed until recently it was what they experienced. The fashionable line to teachers from parents was 'Give them the stick and plenty of it'! All in the Bible, of course. My poem on this subject is 'P.T.A.' in *The Weakness*. This is not a virtue or even a moral position, but I have a fear and loathing of violence that amounts to pathology I think! It makes it impossible to watch Tarantino or those 'Girl with Tattoo' films and so on. I think that dates from country childhood. Arendt's thing about the banality of evil: I think violence is the most banal and depressing form of it. I am full of despair about the readiness of the West – us – to bomb the Middle East, those great cultural centres like Baghdad and Tripoli as a norm of policy nowadays. Violent aggression and assassination seem to be first responses at the beginning of this millennium. Why is nobody objecting?

William Bedford: *Gunpowder* won the 1995 Whitbread Poetry Prize. The dust-jacket talks of these poems drawing 'once more on incidents and episodes' from your upbringing in County Cork, but 'now on a more personal level'. Is that something you were conscious of, perhaps a decision growing out of creative confidence? You must have been encouraged by the way your work was received from the start.

Bernard O'Donoghue: Mystified, is the word. I think when you write in private, on your own, although you have some kind of ideal readership in your head, you don't really imagine anyone else reading what you write. In fact I think it might pervert it if you did. But I have never worked out a gracious way of responding to people who say they have read a poem of mine and liked it. Heaney does it beautifully again: 'God love you!' he says. I don't think that I thought about those poems as more personal either. I think the best poem there 'The Iron-Age Boat' was the most impersonal, the best founded in its landscape.

William Bedford: We do tend to look for 'development' in our writers and artists – rather artificially I think – but I wonder whether you saw this collection in that light?

Bernard O'Donoghue: I didn't really. I often think that people often give credit to the following book as it were: maybe the more substantial stuff in *The Weakness* was rewarded by an accolade to the next book. I like the last poem in *Gunpowder* – 'Metamorphosis' – and that *is* pretty personal.

William Bedford: You quote Norman MacCaig for the epigraph to *Here Nor There*, published 1999: 'Something to do with territory makes them sing.'

And the dust-jacket shows a detail from Bicci Di Lorenzo's *St. Nicholas rebuking the tempest* from the Ashmolean collection. As a matter of interest, three of the four Chatto & Windus collections feature works of Medieval art. You clearly had a say in that decision?

Bernard O'Donoghue: Yes, I chose the pictures and the Chatto designers did a wonderful job with them. The 'St Nicholas' has always been one of my favourite pictures – something that many people in Oxford claim. Someone pointed out that the cropping of the painting means that the mermaid has been cut out, but neither I nor the designer planned that. It may have some significance that we didn't notice though. I think the MacCaig line is wonderful too: birds of course, but it has the same universality as 'The Singer of Tales' – music expressing attachment to place. MacCaig is a marvellous poet: he died the day I got the Whitbread prize which took the shine off it a bit. He was the pride of the Chatto fleet.

William Bedford: With *Here Nor There*, the title, the epigraph, and the Di Lorenzo detail all concentrate our attention on the idea of exile. Well mine, anyway. You've written about Dante as 'the great "inner émigré", the poet of the Ovidian *tristia* of the exile'. Ovid, Dante and Mandelstam are the great examplars of exile. I wonder whether the idea of exile is becoming more central to you with this collection, especially as the opening poem 'Nechtan' has Bran and his companions 'fated/To sail for ever in the middle seas, outcast/ Alike from the one shore and the other'. Am I making too much of this?

Bernard O'Donoghue: Certainly not: you are entirely right. The book is consciously about exile. In fact that was the first of my books that had a coherent overall title I think. The problem might be that I've got a bit stuck in the groove. Everything has been about exile since. It is a capacious subject though: there are so many things we are exiled from – not just place. People, youth... I remember the moment I chose the title and its poem, 'Westering Home', driving west through Wales on the way to Ireland. I liked the rather mannered suppression of the 'Neither' at the start. If 'neither here nor there' means insignificant, then the removal of the negativing word at the start must mean that the surviving bit means not insignificant, therefore important. QED. I suppose I think of exile as a kind of creative privation too, in sharpening emotional consciousness of what has been lost, what we are exiled from. It is largely Ireland of course in my case. The great statement (as often) is Yeats's: 'Does the imagination dwell the most/Upon a woman gained or woman lost?' The imaginative figure in the Tower is 'impatient to be gone': the answer is too obvious to need giving.

William Bedford: *Outliving*, the last of the Chatto & Windus volumes, published in 2003, closes with one of the bleakest poems I think you've published: 'The Mule Duignan'. I'm not clear whose experience is being voiced, but the poem recreates a child's distress at seeing his parents' anxiety, and an adult's anger at a way of life which produces such anxiety:

> I hate that country:
> its poverties and embarrassments
> too humbling to retell. I'll never ever
> go back to offer it forgiveness.

Even if the circumstances are not autobiographical, the feeling seems to be personal. Could you say something about that?

Bernard O'Donoghue: I think you have said it all, William! It is not of course autobiographical, but it is decidedly personal. (I have just written something about this poem in *The Reader*). My friend the Irish builder and musician Mick Henry tell wonderful and heartbreaking stories of the hardships of the lives of the Irish labourers in England in the 1960s and after. One of his most haunting is the story of 'The Mule Duignan' (real nickname). The poem is only a slight elaboration of the narrative exactly as Duignan told the story to Henry; the central declaration 'if the cow does die tonight, we'll have to sell up and go' is verbatim from the narrative. That is partly why it is in speech marks. What I am saying I suppose is that nostalgia is an indulgence. You have to be reasonably well-off and comfortable to feel wistful about the locale of the poverties of your origins. Those labourers were forced out of Ireland by poverty; that is what Duignan does not forgive.

William Bedford: The title *Outliving* clearly invites reflection, and not just on the literal 'outliving' experienced in the first poem, 'The Day I Outlived My Father'. Titles are gifts from writers, or ought to be. I have the sense that you usually have something 'in mind' with your titles?

Bernard O'Donoghue: Yes, particularly since *Here Nor There*: they were slightly more hit-or-miss before that (like *Poaching Rights* which I like as a title, but I am not sure what I meant by it.) I like *Outliving* as a title because I think it encapsulates several things I wanted to say with it. The title poem's sense of 'living longer than'; but also – a bit like the Mule Duignan again maybe – the good fortune of living a higher quality of life: more affluent. Also I suppose living outside the native terrain. I like living in England but I am always slightly abroad here. As I said already, that has positives as well as negatives to it. An early poem called 'The Migrant Workers' (only in *Poaching Rights* I think) is about this:

> There's pleasure in saying 'I live somewhere else;
> My topography is more than meets the eye'.

So 'outliving' is all that too.

William Bedford: Were you translating *Sir Gawain and the Green Knight* whilst teaching the poem? I suppose I'm wondering how a tutorial would differ from the task of translating? Are there two distinct processes going on here with the word translating?

Bernard O'Donoghue: That is interesting. I translated *Gawain* more or less incessantly between 1966 and 2011, so I had a pretty full version in my head before I began the Penguin translation. It was different, yes. A tutorial translation has got to get the full literal sense of the original words – or as near as possible to that. The 'verse' translation aims more at capturing the spirit or implication of the original: the connotation rather than the denotation, or something like that. I found it difficult to bring it to life I think. But that may just be a measure of how much I revere the poem. I found it easier to be satisfied with the bits of *Piers Plowman* I have done (though I revere that too). I think the translation I am least dissatisfied with is 'The Wanderer' in *Farmers Cross*. I think I am not a 'great translator' – unlike Chaucer!

William Bedford: Has Pound's practice as a translator been important to you. Particularly a poem such as 'The Wanderer' and one of my favourites from *Outliving* which isn't actually in the *Selected Poems*, 'Love's Medium.'

Bernard O'Donoghue: Pound really *was* a great translator: in fact I think he was the greatest translator in English since the sixteenth century. What Pound does is to reserve the right to move away from the literal sense of the original, but to keep a full sense of the original's impact in a version that even resolves cruxes of interpretation. His translation of Cavalcanti's '*Donna mi prega*' would be my nomination for the greatest translation of a short poem in English. 'Love's Medium' was written for the wedding of two ex-students of mine. It is loosely based on the Anglo-Saxon 'Wulf and Eadwacer', one of the great obscure love-poems in English (if that is what it is). My poem has a couple of good ideas in it (like the man chopping a tree making wood). I think maybe I thought it didn't hang together well enough to make the *Selected*. But I am glad you like it! It would have provided an opportunity to correct that 'it's'. I suspect that I rejected it for the *Selected* because I was in denial about that possessive mark.

William Bedford: You moved to Faber & Faber with the publication of *Farmers Cross* in 2011, and that volume has an interesting epigraph from Basho: 'Of all the many places mentioned in poetry, the exact location of most is not known for certain.' This is a collection which is full of wanderers and refugees, across cultures and histories. I love the way 'History' has an epigraph from Aelfric's preface to *The Life of King Edmund*, and yet takes us down the years from Abraham Lincoln's funeral to your own childhood and – I assume from the poem's 'you' – the childhood of your own children. This is a long, and moving because so long, historical perspective.

Bernard O'Donoghue: I am very keen on the Basho epigraph. It comes from one of my favourite books (in fact it might be my very favourite book), *Narrow Road to a Far Province,* written in late seventeenth-century Japan and describing the wanderings around Honshu by a couple of poets in old age. The idea is echoed in *Farmers Cross* by Petrarch's *Ascent of Mount Ventoux* from which I have taken the epigraph for my George Watson elegy 'Ascent of Ben Bulben'. As he is getting older Petrarch decides he would like to see the view from the top of Mt Ventoux, but deliberates about who he should travel with, reflecting 'so rare a thing is absolute congeniality in every attitude and habit even among dear friends'. *Farmers Cross* is not about exile as *Outliving* was; it is about ageing: a topic I find increasingly compelling! Travelling in preparation for the end...

William Bedford: I think there is a definite sense of 'first and last things' in *Farmers Cross*. That the poems are not just reflecting on 'life', but your own life. We've already mentioned the theme of exile in the first poem, 'Bona-Fide Travellers', and the last poem is a beautiful elegy to a lost friend, 'The Year's Midnight.' You do have a remarkable gift for letting the visionary shine through the apparently prosaic detail, as in the very last line of this poem: 'and the shades fell not long after 3p.m'. That's a risky dying-fall, but such endings always work with you. You obviously take great care with the arrangement of your collections, the opening and closing poems clearly being very important?

Bernard O'Donoghue: I am glad you think that dying fall gets away with it. I think in books, as with readings, you have to give thought to the first and last items: eschatology again! What comes in between is less crucial. I should say that Matthew Hollis was enormously helpful in arranging the poems in

Farmers Cross. I remember Helen Farish helping a lot with the order too: she suggested putting 'Bona-Fide Travellers' first. That book is very personal, it is true: drifting close indeed to the confessional that I have rather grandly abjured.

William Bedford: Are collections clearly themed in your mind as they develop, or simply accumulations of poems, the themes developing out of the process of writing? I'm thinking of Eliot's remark in 'The Three Voices of Poetry' that he doesn't 'know what he has to say until he has said it'.

Bernard O'Donoghue: Or whoever said 'how do I know what I think until I hear what I say?' It is exactly as you describe: you gather the poems together and see what they amount to by the end: try to impose a collective theme on them. Titles are very crucial I think. Think of things like *The Waste Land* or Yeats's *The Tower* or Heaney's *North*. There are risks of course: titles can be a bit procrustean. When I told John Fuller over the phone that I had settled on *The Weakness* as a title (it was suggested by my daughter Ellie and endorsed by Mick Imlah who was my Chatto editor), John paused briefly and said 'Yes. It's a *brave* title, isn't it?' – which was quite right. I think what is happening now is that my life has caught up with my titles: I rather stymied myself by banging on about death when I was young ('Razorblades and Pencils' and all that), so that it is hard to see where to go after ageing now. 'The only end of age', as Larkin cheerfully says.

William Bedford: It seems to me that your most powerful poems often begin with an ordinary event or anecdote, before opening out into a moment of startling metaphor or epiphany. Assuming you accept the word at all, I wonder whether you understand the idea of epiphany in the traditional religious sense, or as Joyce's secular 'revelation of the whatness of a thing', which always sounds like Hopkins's or Duns Scotus's 'thisness' or *haecceitas* to me?

Bernard O'Donoghue: That is very interesting. I think I like to begin with an event or an image and then see what it can be made to mean. My favourite TV moment of 2011 was the girl in the magnificent *Educating Essex* who said wonderingly 'What is pi? Where does it come from?' – certainly the question of the year. I think my epiphanies are closer to the religious sense than Joyce's (which are mischievously elusive anyway – Gogarty asking to have his sausages delivered. What is *that* about?). It is back to the Anglo-Saxon elegies yet again – 'wisdom and experience': the moral sense that can be drawn from something. Metaphor is part of it too, that's true. The language has to work. I am not confident that mine always does. Everyone knows the occasional moment of triumphantly throwing the pencil on the floor because the last line has come out right. The opposite experience is commoner!

William Bedford: Has the Catholic faith been a continuing part of your life? You've mentioned St Ignatius, St Teresa, *The Cloud of Unknowing*, Evelyn Underhill, Thomas Merton in passing, when talking about Heaney. But a lifetime teaching Medieval literature must have brought you close to Walter Hilton's *The Ladder of Perfection*, Richard Rolle's *The Fire of Love*, Julian of Norwich's *Revelations of Divine Love*, the volumes of Middle English religious prose. It's a rich spiritual and linguistic inheritance.

Bernard O'Donoghue: Yes indeed – not to mention Dante, bizarrely everyone's preferred poet in the post-faith twentieth century. Catholicism has been incalculably important to me of course – I don't know how much it infiltrates everything. Certainly the kind of rich and metaphorical language that I respond to – and the sense of life lived seriously. I think I am not exactly spiritual by disposition though. Maybe seriousness about the world strikes me as the greatest virtue, as I have. We only get one go at life, so we have to make sure it tells.

William Bedford: You have elsewhere asked yourself the question 'what exactly is meant by "an Irish poet"?' It's a complicated question, and I wonder whether you are any the clearer as to an answer?

Bernard O'Donoghue: No, I am not. There are all kinds of unhappy definitions that I don't accept though. An Irish poet is someone born in Ireland who takes Ireland as a subject some of the time. I think Edna Longley's warning is salutary: Ireland is not a good single diet for the Irish poet. But there is so much that is enriching about Ireland: the landscape, its sociology (as represented by Joyce or Frank O'Connor), its mixture of the secular-pagan and the numinous. No, I still don't know. But I am very proud to claim Irishness, poet or not.

William Bedford: We've been talking about the idea of exile, and it is there throughout your poetry and in many of the responses to your poetry. But *Poetry Ireland Review* made the point that although you are clearly 'an Irish émigré poet', your work seems 'refreshingly without the anxieties and hangups of the exiled, displaced expatriate, revelling instead in his freedom to inhabit more than one place.' Your title *Here Nor There* seems an affirmation of that? It would be a fine celebratory note for us to end on.

Bernard O'Donoghue: Yes, I would like to end with that. I am not the best or most experienced citizen of the world, but I do think that living where we are now is the thing to be seized on gratefully, always. Virgil and Dante are very poignant lamenters of the tragic figures who revoked their 'share of sweet life'. The Mule Duignan is maybe wrong to feel bitter about the Ireland of his childhood; but he is right to settle for whatever the here-and-now offers. And *Here Nor There* is meant to be positive in just that way: cautiously rejecting the negative and the insignificant. Best foot forward!

Bibliography

The Courtly Love Tradition (ed.) (Manchester University Press, 1982)

Thomas Hoccleve: Selected Poems (ed.) (Carcanet, Fyfield Books, 1982)

Razorblades and Pencils (Sycamore Press, 1984)

Poaching Rights (Gallery, 1987)

The Absent Signifier (Mandeville, 1990)

The Weakness (Chatto & Windus, 1991)

Gunpowder (Chatto & Windus, 1995)

Seamus Heaney and the Language of Poetry (Harvester Wheatsheaf, 1995)

Here Nor There (Chatto & Windus, 1999)

Oxford Irish Quotations (ed.) (Oxford University Press, 1999)

Outliving (Chatto & Windus, 2003)

Zbyněk Hejda: A Stay in a Sanatorium and other poetry (translator) (Southword Editions, 2005)

Sir Gawain and the Green Knight (translator) (Penguin, 2006)

Selected Poems (Faber & Faber, 2008)

Farmers Cross (Faber & Faber, 2011)

Adam Feinstein

Introduction to two translations of poems by Pablo Neruda on exile

When the Uruguayan critic, Emir Rodríguez Monegal, published his study of the great Nobel Prize-winning Chilean poet, Pablo Neruda, in 1966, he chose to call it: *El viajero inmóvil* (The Immobile Voyager). The title was an apt description of Neruda's life: though a constant traveller, he always longed to be back in Chile. The two Neruda poems I have selected for this special issue of *Agenda* come from Neruda's 1964 collection, *Memorial de Isla Negra* (Isla Negra Notebook). Although Neruda wrote the book in Chile between 1962 and 1964, while living happily with his third wife-to-be, Matilde Urrutia, many of the poems in it recall his tempestuous past.

Madrid, the subject of the first poem here, was the setting for the key transformation of Neruda's poetry from one of self-absorbed anguish to an outward-looking weapon for social and political justice. As Chilean Consul in the Spanish capital from 1934, Neruda had witnessed the horrors of Spain's Civil War and the shocking murder of his great friend, Federico García Lorca, in August 1936. The opening lines of this poem allude to the fact that, officially, at least, Neruda could not, and would not, return to Spain while General Franco was in power. In fact, he *did* return secretly – and fleetingly – on several occasions before Franco's death in 1975 – but significantly only to coastal regions (the Canary Islands, Cádiz, Barcelona) rather than to his beloved Madrid. He never did see his friend - the Spanish poet, Vicente Aleixandre - again. By the time Aleixandre won the Nobel Prize for Literature in 1977, Neruda was dead.

The second poem is Neruda's depiction of the restlessness of exile. He himself was forced to flee from Chile in 1949 following his courageous condemnation of President Gabriel González Videla's dictatorial régime. After escaping across the Andes on horseback, he spent three years in Europe before returning to Chile to a hero's welcome in 1952.

Adam Feinstein's biography, Pablo Neruda: *A Passion for Life*, was published by Bloomsbury in 2004.

Pablo Neruda

Oh, My Lost City

I loved Madrid but I will never
see it again, never. That's
the bitter truth and it fills me
with despair. I feel as though I died
along with those I loved, as if
half my soul went to its grave
and lay under the dry plains
with prisons and prisoners,
before the flowers were stained with blood
and the moon wore clots of red.

I loved the outskirts of Madrid,
the streets slipping away to Castile
like little, dark-eyed rivers.
It was the end of the day:
alleys lined with ropework and casks,
esparto plaited like heads of hair,
arched staves of barrels
from which
some day
wine would fly to a rowdy new home;
streets of coal
and lumberyards
and taverns overflowing
with torrents of that
harsh Valdepeñas wine.

I walked the lonely streets,
mute and packed dry as adobe.
I was lost without an alphabet or a guide.
I neither searched nor found,
just lived my life,
joining the clods of earth in their silence,
joining the stones in their fever.

Then all was quiet at last:
no more wails from windows,
no more singing from a well,
no more roars of laughter
to shatter the dusk
with a slice of glass.
And even closer: in the throat
of the city at night,
dusty horses,
red-wheeled carts,
the aroma of bakeries at closing time,
and the nocturnal petals
as I headed vaguely towards
Cuatro Caminos, to Number 3,
Calle Wellingtonia.
Waiting for me there were
eyes like sparks of blue
and the smile I'll never see again:
Vicente Aleixandre. I left him there,
with his rosy, full moon face,
to live with his dead friends.

Exile

Surrounded by castles of weary stone,
strolling the beautiful streets of Prague,
meeting smiles and Siberian birches.
Or on Capri, ablaze in the sea,
with the scent of bitter rosemary.
And then came love. Yes, love
made generous peace with me.
Yet all the while,
two friendly hands
were carving a dark hole
in the stone core of my soul
and there my country burns for me,
summons me, yearns for me, urges me
to keep on living, to endure the worst.

Exile is round in shape:
a circle, a ring.
Your feet walk in circles, across land
which isn't even yours.
You're woken by the light,
and the light's not yours.
Night falls, but without the stars.
You find brothers, but they're not of your blood.
You're like a blushing ghost, ashamed:
why can't you warm to those who love you?
And it still feels odd to crave
the hostile prickles of your homeland,
the raucous abandon of your own people,
the acrid problems lying in wait
with a snarl at your door.

It was inevitable: my heart clung
to every pointless sign,
as if only the sweetest honey
nestled in the branches of my homeland.
I longed for the faintest trill
of a bird, for the thrill
of the song that roused me
from my sleep
in the damp glow of childhood.

I have always preferred the desolate soil
of my own nation – the craters, the sand,
the mineral gaze of the deserts –
to the glass they filled with light to toast me.
I felt lost, alone in my garden:
I was a rustic boor: the statues
were my enemies – so, too,
everything the centuries had forged
with the symmetry of silvery bees.

Distance clogs so thick
in exile. We breathe in air
through a gaping wound.
There is nothing more unjust
than a rootless soul
turning its back on beauty,
seeking martyrdom and serenity
in one place only:
that unhappy land called home.

Translations by **Adam Feinstein**

Alexandra Petrova

i

One more country to learn. Another page to turn
where I'm a wanderer. I'll ask the green-eyed
gardener to drink up
across the barbed wire
from a one-shot paper cup.

I'll not manage to play the host
and even out in the air the border of the broken
edge burns like a wound: glances, words. After
me like a comma in a curved vector
there's just dust and the plastic trash on died-out sites,
which like me too are chased by the burning wind.

ii

Even if it's only in a dream let me see that island
where there are fountains and rivers. Thunderstorms
had torn out the window frames into the yard outside
from the room with the cool dark parquet floor.
Deep inside the cross-beams were shaking from the light.
And there was an intermittent conversation in the twilight.

Why let oneself go to scalding Egypt?
The baptism crucifix was forgotten it seems
in the little room over the split-veined stream.
You see, Mandelstam's right, 'the air is drunk up'
and even tears lust for thirst.

iii

Transparent morning. The gecko is frozen just so.
The veins of trees are highly strung,
the cicadas ring out and the grasshoppers and the roses and their stems,
and if you succeed in getting out of the shade
then you too will be from all sides
the transparent planet of its venous system.

But the spirit of movement and growth
will cunningly waft over the scythed meadow and the anemones,
this hour at dawn for all the homeless
is only a floating island, only a floating hull.

Translated by **Richard McKane**

Marina Boroditskaya

There is a tree

There is a tree. Its name escapes me.
A prose-like name, it flirts
With poetry, wears poetic oddity.
Ballad of a prison yard. A Japanese birch tree.

Its slender trunk bore a bark of bronze.
It grew in my friend's garden where
On days that seem barely gone
We made hideaways of folding chairs

And a boy, bronze-skinned as an Indian
Vanished as he clutched the tree
And swarmed upwards, sending
A circle trembling through the canopy.

Fourteen years old and travelling light
At the ravine we grazed our herd of bikes
The radio hissed. And somewhere very far
Invisible tanks slid into Prague.

If not for tender little breasts
At the least touch aching –
We'd have pressed ourselves to the smooth bark
And caught the earth quaking

There is a tree. Its name escapes me.
And yet like a chill dark shadow
Like a child's first shameful thoughts
It lies deep in a stranger's meadow.

And if that trunk was felled long ago
Leaving only a trace of sap on its tomb
Then I kiss in my dreams the rings cut through
And all their history enwombed.

A dream

My poor spirit stands before
The heavenly medical board
Sight: shit, muscle tone: slight
Hearing: flawed
Naked, weighed and measured,
A trembling fool
Upon whom the narrowed eyes
Of the recruiting archangel fall.

The mysterious, the glorious
St Michael, the battle-scarred
Asks only one question:
'Soldier, did you fight hard?'
'Well... I put my best foot forward...
I piped my pipe... Woke men's hearts...
And I... I never expected any reward
Ask Gabriel there – he'll take my part'.

You wandered in a haze! You sprawled and lazed!
You mucked about
Dozed in the sun, half-dazed
Cloud-gazed.
Those heights you were to gain
From the dark – they were beyond you!
You will wake as a woman again
With winter upon you.

Exodus

So I was wondering how they crossed that seabed
When the whole watery firmament was combed, wave to floor
And the squelch, squelch, squelch, and the walls on either side
Going up and up like a great aquatic corridor

The babies were carried, the older children, I'm sure
Fell behind, shouting: Look! Look what I've found!
Was it really possible to walk the watery course
Without stopping once to lift a shell's pink round?

What wonders they must have seen on that bed!
The tentacles that jutted from the walls like booms
And yet not all of them knew why they fled
Nor remembered that behind them lay their doom.

And when the prophet Mariam beat on her tambour
And the sea walls bent, and with a tidal roar
Crushed the Egyptians, their horses, swept, destroyed –
Did they shudder, even briefly, before they danced for joy?

Translated by **Sasha Dugdale**

Melisa Gürpinar

An Asian Woman

What a shame,
the times of love
when a western breeze
caressed my hair
are gone,
erased from my notebook.

Now if I say
that one face of the dream chevalier
glows
while his other face slowly darkens
and his looks
rub salt in my wounds,
do you hear
the moans
of an Asian woman?

I may be the first
of anyone to see
the exuberant rise
of the sun
the source of light,
but mapped on the roads of exile
no trace of my footprint appears.
For I am a woman
my rose tree always greens
in the world's back yard.

Besides
I've written poems
all my life
in shame and shyness
I dressed a naked life with words,
I took and left it
on a windy corner.

And if I say,
that waking up
one of those hazy mornings
as an Asian
a woman
a poet
is to be hanged three times
from the same unlucky tree
with the same hangman's rope,
do you believe my words?

Woman's Fate

I came from afar,
dead-beat.
So many thousand years
my journey lasted.
Once upon a time
love was my horse
my dowry legends.
On the strings of a saz
my voice roamed from land to land.
I passed by so many battles
a good many feasts,
if I'd written it all
the rocks would scarcely contain my story.

I came from the steppe
letters in my saddlebag,
with sand and salt and sweet-smelling herbs ...
When sunlight a spear's length
rose on the skyline
I let my hair loose
and from mountain to mountain
I raced
the lowering clouds.

I was woman,
I was fertility's self.
I was light, I was water,
I was the ruler
of winds.
I was the mother
her name known in the world
who gave birth to sons
and daughters with violet eyes
and teeth like pearls,
once upon a time
their loves were woven,
worked in the hearts of all.

Fate turned my life around,
destiny's blow
came down on my head.
Creatures called human
wrapped me in rough sackcloth
sold all my wealth,
cut off my nose and mouth
and threw me in the lake.
It's the law, they said,
it's honour.
I was left adrift
with my sins
on a far-stretching road
between heaven and hell.

Inscribed on my forehead
was woman's fate, it seemed,
thinking it predestined
none could erase it
until today.
But a little lark
now sings
my unfinished song,
pouring its voice on the void.

From the Turkish of Melisa Gürpınar. 2008

Translated by **Ruth Christie**

Birhan Keskin

Sulukule 2008

Write! When the mango trees start to fruit
Write! When good songs land good words
Write! Even a little sentence.
And say; our hearts are jumpy as a primate's.

Write! The world's heading somewhere, and won't return!
Write! We must suffer a thousand troubles before we die.
Write! Just a very short sentence.
And say; the green plums loosen their hold.

Write! There's a smell of fire on the aubergine
Write! Our lives taste like a still life.
Write! Us? Singing songs? No way!
And say; one plant of cyano-bacteria is more than enough!

Write! They bolted the stable door but the horses had fled!
Write! My home has become a winter, my child, in the heart of a dark
continent.
Poets can never write freely of things as they are
But you can, you must! though they'll take no notice.

Write! My home has become a winter, my child

My home reduced to a shambles!

Note: the title refers to the shocking demolition of a lively gypsy neighbourhood in
Istanbul to make way for speculators' high-rise blocks.

Baghdad

Before daybreak. Even before the dawn-chorus
The sky still silent, the tree asleep,
The figtree guarding the roof
While the alyandos and lemon-tree are far away.
Before the water cools in the garden, and notes are made
Before a decision taken, a decision followed
While words are asleep in the dark, before talking begins,
While the chimney knows no flame, before soot and smog set in,
Bird wings are not yet open to flight or diving
There's no umbrella-word, but only leaves
And a dusky purple neither night nor morning.

There are no sighs and cries yet, no seagulls that swoop on the streets
No one wishing for winter's descent on the streets
No one complaining that summer's not yet over.

Aerodynamics don't exist, quantum was never heard of,
The branch not broken, nor the root at war with itself.
Everyone's home is still where they grew up
And no one even asks the meaning of 'home'.
Desire so innocent and childlike
While those who gathered at our first dry well
Haven't yet learned to say, 'We came into the world and must leave it'.

Like morning and evening in short, like morning and evening
Already one within. The world still a warm nest
asleep beneath you, while no one has any suspicion
So innocent, so pure,
Before the split, one half of us still with the other,
When suddenly out of the blue,
Why do they bomb us, Figen,
Why Baghdad?

Gaza

I can't leave you and go elsewhere.
We were wind and shade,
Rain and sleep to each other.
In desolate barges
Whenever you remember
Love me.

It's cloudy in Gaza, seventeen degrees.
Humidity 16 per cent, wind 13 k.p.h.
The nineteenth day of attack, the twentieth night,
Over a thousand dead, thousands wounded.

Now before me I've put four desert photographs.
Four figures of speech to the cold, bloody world
We have poets to speak with feeling, says
Such an asshole on TV about Gaza.

Love me twice in rain in snow in hail,
In your hands I'm a sentence upside down.
Sometimes even a thousand cries can't prevent
The tyrant's ongoing cruelty,
You saw
I too am riddled with holes.

They're bandaged in nylon and rags before they grow up...
Before they grow up, O god I can't look,
Can't look at them... with bullets
These children shot
Horrrrribly, god.

Human, talking of humans,
what's human?
The devil's the one that's lame.

Translated from the Turkish of Birhan Keskin
by **Ruth Christie** *and* **Selçuk Berilgen**

44

Ziba Karbassi

Resistance

Wings shoulder bones wings broken bones
Feather feather feather shorn hair
No more no more colour in her face
No more colour on the face she has at all

No, nothing whatsoever of this world
From your world nothing whatsoever at all
She doesn't even know her own name now
She doesn't even know her own name no
Full of bruises her eyes swollen by blows
Bruises on the thighs her skin torn
Liver in ashes
With all of this pain
All that's left of her is a scream, a scream
And so – she screams

I am daughter of the first mysteries
Secrets, centuries, origins
I am deaf dumb blind
She screams
I'm dumb
And know nothing of nothing

I who stitch threadspans of stars
On the draped robe of night
And put make up on the face of the moon
I who am laughter yes laughter
Haaa the laughs I have haaa
A haa come from my scream haaa
And again and again and a third gain
Til I can take now more and then again
As far as I can go : quick, count the lashings
Ten by ten bone by bone blackened even
     unto blackout

Wings shoulder bones wings broken bones
Feather feather feather shorn hair
No more no more colour in her face
No more colour on the face she has at all

Nothing of nothing she has
                         Nothing to tell you
She knows not her own name doesn't know it at all
No she doesn't she doesn't even know her own name
But yours she knows O yours she knows –
You pimp-fucker – she knows yours
                    very well

Lesgi-Dance

Lesgi that blade shudders grenade pins
lesgi that shatter stomps grapes into wine
that cuts the deck of earth & explodes love
that fountains the dream into its language
– language that tricks out its own dream –
and the fall & rise of throat breath, lesgi
on the top & back of the air flares, lesgi
inside clerical weapons & criminal sham
inside chemical weapons & crimson blood
lesgi .. gi .. go grow to the height of breath
heave the devil's tail up its own backside
head-butt your head on death's forehead
rub your shoulders on the cold air, lesgi
pure heart matter pulsing and pumping
stamp a one-step-forward two-back dance
sit dance sleep softer than soil-fallen rain
hailstones & wolverines kneeing into stone
slapping pain on calm's tender balm, lesgi
a girl's eye on the frontline cobraing right
a young guy sleeving away hidden poisons
bitterness on the rim and lining of the cup
there at the roundtable of bluebirds, lesgi
with listening devices there in all corners
with camera babes sat round their tables
with king & clown & killer, lesgi
– you're deer & tiger & forest – lesgi
– you leap on sabre & broken glass – lesgi
ever straining one neck higher than before
sufi of all dancers, my young sufis – lesgi
there at the height of the minaret – lesgi
the swung censer of the high altar – lesgi
circling spun dancer between sun & time,
& poem-breath from Shams' azure roots,
lesgi – from life to life dance, lesgi, dance,
   live & don't die, lesgi, don't ever die

Translated by **Stephen Watts** *and* **Ziba Karbassi**

47

Adnan al-Sayegh

I Emerged From The War Unawares

I emerged from the age of betrayals
Towards a noble weeping for a green homeland
Ploughed up by pigs and tank tracks
I entered the orbit of the poem
Half free
And half in shackles
So the lamentations are down to you & your hired mourners
And there is nothing for me to do but point out to you
With Na'ilah's fingers
The country's shirts slung across tribal spears
Perforated by gunshot
So the Euphrates will seep bloodily through your fingers
As you write

– All that poets write is in vain
. . . .

For this age teaches us
To applaud the murderers
As they wade the pavements of our blood
And this age teaches us
To diminish ourselves
. . . . . . so the winds may flow freely & keep
Pace with herds gone to summer pastures
But I . . . .
From out of the wreckage the cannons left behind
Will raise my palm, covered by blood-drenched dust . . .
In front of the eyes of the age
I'll teach it how we finger-nail our names
So the word NO will glow out
We who have come out from the barracks
To shake such metropolitan flies off our wounds
Can we be wrong – as such huge lorries pass us –
At the number of martyrs gone off as bombs
And the number of friends

Left queuing to die
But I – the poem the censor's eye has not yet seen –
Am not mistaken about this bitter pain
When we get to the dread of the mothers
Nailed down on railway platforms
Asking those going off to war

To take their nightlong 'kerchiefs
Of tears to dress the wound of distance
Between the bullets & their prayers

They endure the patience of years
Facing vacant, empty beds
In field hospitals … hanging the shrouds of
The dead over wind-swept wash-ropes
So they'll be dry for those next in line …
…………………

Where shall we take our lives – still so tender –
O Lord …….
I will stifle this clamour in my throat
While you breakfast on tea & papers
I will write about a moon that is rising &
About a cloud passing over our wheat-fields

To settle over our wounds
I will soothe your sufferings
So I can move on like a line of the poem
Threading my heart through the alleyways
I will sew the shirt of exile to the size of your sorrows
And leave the blood of my slashed shirt
As my witness & evidence
Before the writer of justice
I've not been defeated …
Nor have I fled – like my cousin's horses –
From the field of battle
The distance of truth between me & the bullets
And this poem, its voice hoarse
From too much hunkering through the trenches
& screaming out in terror & bewilderment :
– Stop beating these drums

Who will delete from my memory tunnels
The images of friends gone away
With neither flower nor slumber
Leaving nothing but my heart's address
Friends who lost the way
To their tears & homes
Friends of the bombs
I have grown old
Before my time
Haven't you seen my lungs blackened by slogans ?
Haven't you seen my body hunkered beneath medal-grabbers ?
O .... what does this heart hide ! ...
What do the young women & newspapers reveal
Those duping their lovers up lifts to pulsing apartments
Greetings to the country of wheat
Greetings to the country of running waters
Greeting to my country, the one that – besieged by bombs –
Carried its wounds like a battle banner
And rebelled against the authority of the Romans
No Romans now but our own countrymen, ready
to back-stab us with their treacherous blades
....
....

A withered tree on my lips and the passing Euphrates has not quenched my
thirst. Behind me the barking of futile wars unleashed on our flesh by the
General, so that we'll have to evade their teeth and the shrapnel that used
to comb the hair of our children before they left for school & roses. I run,
run, through the forests of death, gathering as kindling those gone in the
autumn of battle, on the look-out like a sad star, they left me here alone,
biting down the tip of my dishdasha, dodging my death between bombs
and martyrs. I am a poet whose life has been eaten by words, so how am I
to put these letters together so as to release a sentence, without letting my
heart slip – bewildered – from my tongue so a landmine will explode. I run,
my heart on my motherland : Where will she bury her sons ? ... This earth
smaller than my mother's tears, I'll shake the bullets off my son's skin & he
gathers them in the flour bin. Winds pass through the strings of my heart,
and sorrow in the meadow sings. Butterflies pass over our wounds, then
fly toward flowers. You trees, whose buds have taught us to sprout branches
from our suffering for the spring to come that jasmine will open its windows.
If only the jasmine & my heart would be reasonable ! She takes refuge in his

coat – as war planes fly over – feels his pulse spring-bursting like the garden, brushing the corolla beneath her wet shirt. I lo..ve .. yo..u ! .. Sirens pull her away and kisses are scattered on the grass, earthworms plough them down deep & to jasmine & heart-sorrow. We hang what is left of anger on the hook of war, night comes down over the houses, peaceful in the vagueness of evening & bitter lilies, birds descend over warehouse roofs, a flock of cranes veer into my soul's spring. Tomorrow in a dawn without warplanes, we'll run under drizzling violets, we'll melt together ... we'll wander through streets of laughter, we'll stroke the fountain's hair. I will recall that your hands loved to slumber in my hands, and we will grow, does the field grow from a flower ... or from your hands ? I will see what I see of love's madness on her breast, my soul carried off like a lark, I will gather flowers from her dress & from meadows mowed by shrapnel. Honeys pouring from the lips' error make me stagger ... was it an error to love ? The alley that brought us together in the pine trees' shade remembers how my heart stole your breast with-out my hands noticing .... had I drunk too much ? ... But don't convince me you're warmer than the land, this country is at a bomb's distance from your veins & you a migrant bird among dictionaries. We measure life with the calibre of a grenade, as it arcs across our long-suffered patience, we'll subtract it from the excess of shrapnel and wear it like a shirt of impossible, absurd joy, so

> Is it
> wrong
>   that we
>   so love
>   Life !? ...
>
>   ......

Baghdad: December 14th 1991

51

This Pain ... That Shines

I'm just sat down – on a sunny day –
My legs crossed, the ones buckled by war
Folded in by the maelstrom of the street that will bring me postcards
                                    from lost friends & idleness

Fast buses & clouds of unknowing

Recounting for your melancholic eyes the long history of my sorrows
When in the blink of one eyelid
Images of bombs start falling instead of tears
Enough of this gazing into my eyes ...
I've already wept too much, more than I should
More than the amount of tears allotted my life

And now ...
I have to smile in front of the mirrors of this splendid restaurant that
        my astonished feet have just now walked me into

Folded in by your bare arms ...

While precious wraps half-uncover other alluring customers
Allow me – just a few moments –
While this anxiety inhabiting me subsides

Since I – accidentally – found the credit card of your tenderness

Allow me – just a few hours –

So that inside me the years of mud & restlessness & bullets
That the foreign waiter's cloth cannot wipe off – he's nudging me
                                            very politely
So he can remove the drops of coffee that in my confusion I spilt
Over the table's white cloth –
I should have told you, at the very least & before anything else,
About the gardens of my childhood ploughed by the teeth of bulldozers &
tanks
And about my heart that still trembles on the pavements whenever it comes
across

what remotely resembles her long hair

About the bombs the recollection of which is dug into my face
About the women of the salons who snigger at the sight of my mud-
splattered boots
About the pavements that banished me during my short times of leave
(clandestine, stolen times)

And the trees that hid in the pores of my skin during the bombardments
About the bitter years the taste of which stayed stuck to my lip ... until now
Until this moment of your pineapple juice & my cup of coffee
Enough of your staring into the mirrors of my eyes.

I know ... I know ... I know

I know that ...
These memories have ruined my life completely
I know, these poems that were mired with me in the swamps
And that I carried in bunkers, cafes & down narrow border tracks
Will stay with me wherever I set off for
I know, this heart will squander whatever's left of me
Already I'm tangled up there ...

Completely enmeshed ...

And in spite of this I would not have wanted
To change my life for any other :
I am the owner of this pain that shines.

Baghdad: late 1980s

Translated by **Marga Burgui-Artajo** *and* **Stephen Watts**

A.N. Stencl

from 'Whitechapel Idyll'

ix

Thousands of little chimneys on the roofs about
Smoke from our home must be from one of them?
On the washing-lines wet ones flap in the wind:
A familiar little nappy swaying against the sky?

Because your eyes already are black-glittering
Nothing else seems as if it matters any more!
If we cannot go back to our own home shtetl
Maybe we can bring it here to where we are –

x

Mama's whispering lips I only saw when she
Lit the holy Shabes candles: I looked at them,
At their quiet trembling and even now I know
And understand how God can be talked to.

Was it my Mama, or because I was then a child
That poor room filled with secret done in light?
I can see him in your eyes: you teaching him
How to speak with human lips to God –

xi

Dark little courtyards, and shadowed in dark
Reflected in Shabes-calm the whole week long
Each tiny street is a lit-up bridge like this:
We'll go across it happily toward the Messiah

Our own heaven weaving itself onto the street
With 'Kedushe' and 'Borkhu' & then 'Amen'
Accompanied by the joy-song of the sewing feet
Its 'Three Seamstresses' and its 'Dear Little Son' –

54

A light-lit tiny smile from my father's eyes
Which then loses itself inside his thick beard –
How beautiful his whole life in his lit face! –
I will find it when I'm old and full of years.

In his religious books it was quietly hidden
With each grey hair placed between the pages
As if such hairy rootlets in lines of tilled soil
Could juice and mature it down all the ages –

xv

And if, God forbid, we'd run away from home
Like a needed shtetl we'd take you off with us
As if from Poland, Lithuania, you Whitechapel –
I rhythm-sense the run-rhyme move my feet!

From the charnel-pit as an unextinguished spark
A little Shabes candle leaves the house from here
We'll carry it somewhere far-off with bare hands
And bring it home before it dies wholly down …

Translated by **Khayke Beruriah Wiegand** *and* **Stephen Watts**

Daniele Serafini

A Distant Venice

In Memory of Carlotta Z

'And somewhere at the bottom he fell into darkness. That much he knew. He had
fallen into darkness. And at the instant he knew, he ceased to know'.

Jack London: *Martin Eden*

i

For you water proved
at first companionship
then destiny
lagoon and river
offering birth
then oblivion
your brief lifetime
darkened
beneath a bridge
one autumn still echoing
that change of mind
that scream for help
too late before the last
and fatal swirl of water.

You'd grown up wearing
a sad smile and a look of pride
walking head high
between San Polo and the waterfront –
grave, sedate, those early
shadows already on your face.

ii

You loved embroidery,
delicate fingerwork
uncompleted like words

that leave no trace,
sunsets over the Lido.

You loved with fierce
possessiveness –
isolated, isolating –
unable to decide
among your store of trinkets,
Flemish miniatures or the scores
of music never played.

Venice became the bitter season
soon a mere memory
forgotten later in the slow
inertia of those muffled rooms
close to the castle of Colloredo
haunted by the light
footsteps of the lovers
in that novel – your ghosts,
your nightly companions.

Then, unexpectedly,
the clash of arms,
a sneak attack, soldiers,
tears shed, exhausted horses,
days spent with wind and mud

iii

then a fresh smell
of dairy-farms and wheat –
a string of villages
Melegnano, Crema, Ombriano –
ending up in poverty
at Romanengo.

Here, years of hard
earth, parched earth, a land
of mulberry-trees and solitude,
your sons, those silences, a distant Venice –
and through the smoke of burning stubble

a harsher feeling of life,
a hoarse lament about exile
reducing to sepia all
memories of pallid water,
canals, marshes, islands
like Pellestrina or Torcello,
the dome of San Giorgio Maggiore –
places gone so remote
just images and sounds
all shattered in the hollow
quality of grief.

But water summoned
like a duty,
as nursemaid, tyrant,
in that October
heralding the end.

iv

And one day you no longer knew
whether it was a canal
or a lagoon which seized you
so ferociously –
the current dragging,
the whirlpool distorting,
the river offering
eternal future,
altering voice, eyes, fate
to light of pure redemption
from domes, from crosses,
from cramped familiar squares –
then peace at last
graveyard on San Michele
only the fluttering of marsh-birds
and the suspended beating
of your weakened heart.

Venezia lontana

Translated by **Harry Guest**

Jordi Doce

Without Title

I don't quite know what we talked about
nor why...
Perhaps only the night
said things that made sense,
withdrawn a few steps
against the wailing wall.
We others broke the ice
sharing cigarettes and rhetorical questions.
Thin weeds, scars of dry land,
the paltry warmth of the poppy
breathing beneath the tongues of the sleepless.
I don't know what exactly we said
nor what for...
The world slipped away outside the camp
but no watch realized.
The dogs, the horses,
drowsed in shifts
and their snores let us recognize ourselves.
Why does no one remember now?
Hunger and cutting cold.
Under the unsatisfied moon
just words and words.

Translated by **Lawrence Schimel**

Norbert Hirschhorn

Sleep my child

My life, my only Kaddish,
    your father's in America where
        people eat challah even weekdays.

    lyu-lyu-lyu

                Ludlow Street, tenement,
                    filthy room, that's where
                       your father lives.

He'll send us twenty dollars,
    he'll send his picture too. Someday,
        he'll send for us, America.

    lyu-lyu-lyu

                Starved, weak, soup kitchens:
                stale bread, no meat,
                  he feeds on smoke.

I'll make for you some
    chicken soup while we wait
        for the happy letter.

    lyu-lyu-lyu

                Layoffs, a bitter time. He has to
                come home, has to
                  borrow for the boat.

Your mother sits by your cradle
    and cries. One day, you'll know
        what she really meant.

    lyu-lyu-lyu

A recomposition blending two lullabies; one by Sholem Aleichem (1859-1916),
'Shlof Mayn Kind' ('Sleep my child'; the other an untitled response by Michl
Kaplan (1881-1944); both lyrics and literal translations from Ruth Rubin's 'Voices
of a People. The Story of Yiddish Folksong' (Urbana and Chicago: University of
Illinois Press, 2000; p. 40 and p. 362). A musical rendition is at www.youtube.com/
watch?v=8YnsKnXE7Dg.

A Czarist Conscript Bids Farewell

Be well, dear parents,
I'm off to a far away place –
Windless, where no bird sings,
No rooster cries the morning.

Cry not, dear parents,
But forgive your son
If he does not keep kosher –
Pig and potatoes is what they serve.

Stay whole, dear parents,
Even as I leave you. May
God grant you well-being

All the years of your lives.

A recomposition of the folksong, 'Zeyt gesunterheyt', by S. Ginsburg and P. Marek (1901). From Yidishe Folkslider' compiled by M. Beregovsky and A. Fefer Kiev, USSR: Melokhe Ferlag, 1938, p. 265. Reproduced digitally by National Yiddish Book Center, Amherst, MA. The original song was a bride's farewell to her parents. For a description of conscription of Jews under the Czars see http:// grossmanproject.net/Military%20Conscription.htm.

The Wandering Jew

Bundle on a stick, satchel
on my back. What

else do I need? What else? A hut with
seven kids, a goat, and seven

kopeks, what else do I need? The rain
slaps against the window, beggars

whistle down the chimney.
What? What else do I need? Lost

my moxie, down on luck, I jump from
rabbi to rabbi, not one helps.

Who needs? Who needs you?

A recomposition of a traditional folksong, 'Ikh Nem Dos Pekl' ('I take the pack')
found on www.zemerl.com; no attributions given.

Gëzim Hajdari

i

For you men of Europe who scrape by each day,
for you women of the East who scrub floors or walk
the old people of the West around the block for fresh air,
for you immigrants who sleep on benches & wake up
immeasurably homesick,
for you dossers who'll have no bosses
& live in peace with the universe,
for you prostitutes who offer your sex to
black men white men yellow men
up to blood-point,
for you blind people forsaken in deepest eternal dark,
for you sick & out of work as solidarity & mercy,
for you missionaries comforting the weak before death,
for you peasants who graze your herds &
plough the fields from north to south,
for you mad people who give us free tuition in madness,
for you who are alone & fugitive like me
I write these verses in Italian
& torment myself in Albanian.

ii

In which season do I look for you,
from which stone do I call out to you,
on which snow do you walk.

You are what's left inside me of a summer night,
green grass grown in the burnt field,
beautiful as the spring in Darsia.

In you light rises, darkness falls,
I cover you with gorse flowers & blackbird songs,
all present & future days unfold
through the pathways of your fingers.

No matter the language in which I dream of you
you are the same: body & time,
you singing of your childhood like you once did:
from hill to hill, let me roam you
like a goatherd.

iii

I leave these verses as a farewell
swallowed by the nakedness of memory
knowing that the world has no use for them.
Of the greeting I send with a shaking hand,
down there in the starry depths,
no one's aware.
Precarious horizon
I'm leaning on your cold water
& excavating your forehead of dark sky.

Forsaken in the thick fog
I don't know where I come from or where I'm going.
I lay siege to snows that besiege me
at the mercy of dark birds.
I want to know who keeps me away from an insane land
& what will be the end of my Shadow beyond the water,
of the rain that falls in the rain
of the gods among the trees.

Standing in line next to cold weather next to destiny
I wait to be called at daybreak from the stones
by wan faces of hoarsened voices.

My name a line dividing
light from darkness,
my body a border between sand & sky.

iv

Thirsty kiss, snow that lays siege to me,
stars without mouths to light your orphaned blindness.
I've come from the parched line of the horizon & I can see
men and birds embracing over there.

64

Why is it that Time is short & the rains won't call us back?
Advance my blood towards dark woods,
depart my Voice towards the hymn of stones and glorify the sky
spread over my wild skin.
It's fire comes after me from ocean to ocean,
can you see how it advances and burns my ancient footprints
so as to birth new ashes?

v

Each day in exile I create a new homeland
in which I die & am reborn,
a homeland without any maps or flags
celebrated by your deep eyes
that chase after me all the time
on the journey towards fragile skies.
In every land I sleep as a man in love,
in every house I wake up as a child,
my key can unlock every border and
the doors of each & every black prison.
Returns & eternal departures my being
from fire to fire, from water to water.
My homelands' anthem: the blackbird's song
that I sing at every season of waning moon
risen from your forehead of darkness & stars
with the eternal will of the Sun god.

vi

Tonight I wait to be calmed by snow on the border,
the sea of sand, faces in the water.
No other sky in which to sink my derangement
everywhere the night of dying men.

Where shall I stop, my terror,
the stones I've thrown against the wind
have opened over me measureless chasms.

Now time abides in time
& I walk through room after room, wall after wall.
I'm an exile exiled into exile
my blood shed on the trees & my voice in the rain.

Do you know my pain? I walk side by side with those
who feel their way along a tightrope that's catching fire.
Advance, advance two-headed black eagles, devour anew
my shredded body, noose my red heart to the branches,
drink up my blood like ravening beasts,
bury my songs,
just leave me time enough to cover
this daily childhood.

Alas, the future full fathom five,
the past in the black of the world.

Translated by **Cristina Viti**

Cristina Viti in Conversation with Gëzim Hajdari

Can you say something about your cultural background?

My cultural background – luckily – belongs to the last century. I grew up with Albanian epic songs. As a teenager, I would read every night before sleep the borderland folk songs celebrating the deeds of *shqiptar* (Albanian) warriors as they defended their people and their border – my favourite was *The Marriage Of Halìl*. So I am for the ancient flavour of things. I come from the Northern Alps, the mystical place of the Bjeshkët and the Nëmuna (known as 'the Cursed Mountains'). For centuries they have been like a huge stage set for one of the most majestic and cruel tragedies of human history, stained by the blood of mountain people (the *malësori*). Valleys, streams, wood, water springs, summits and caves were guarded by Oreads, Fairies and Pixies, as in pagan times. And it is precisely the Bjeshkët and Nëmuna that were ruled by the *Kanun* (the oral Code of Justice). The north of Albania was self-governed on the basis of the Kanun for five hundred years. Every aspect of daily life, from birth to death, rested on the Kanun. Everything happened through the word. The reason why my ancestors moved to the central area of the country was the need to keep the continuity of the family safe from the *hasmëria,* or blood feud. The people of northern Albania, the fiercest of the nation, who were often forced to face attacks from invading powers to defend Albania's identity and integrity, opposed the Ottoman invasion with armed resistance. Not being subjected to the Turkish administration, they decided to govern themselves through the *besa*, or 'given word', 'promise'. Laws, marriage vows, honour, truce, revenge, hospitality and songs were all transmitted orally from father to son, generation to generation. For us Albanians, the word is holy and sacred. The word must never be trifled with. Despite their Catholic faith, the people of the Cursed Mountains make vows in the name not of God, but of the *besa*.

Later I became familiar with Albanian lyrical poetry, the lyrical folk songs of the *nizam* (as the Albanian soldiers fighting for the Sublime Porte of Istanbul were known in Turkish) and the songs of the *kurbet* (migrant workers). These were sung by the men of my village at festivals or weddings, and are of extraordinary beauty, unique in the Balkans and unrivalled in the history of European poetry. So I am indebted to the Albanian epic tradition.

Beside the Chinese classics, the Arab mystics and the Russian symbolists, I also love the French 'maudits' and the English 'Romantics' such as Byron, Keats and Shelley.

The orality of Albanian tradition has had a very deep influence on your poetry ...

Yes: the history of Albania is shaped by the tragedies that have marked the character, soul and spirit of the Albanian people to the core, and has a very rich oral tradition, in which the collective memory of a nation is mirrored and preserved. Albanian orality has a terrible beauty, tragic and deeply moving: the cruel, indelible beauty enclosed in our souls as a consequence of our history and of our tragedy, dating back to remote, dark times. To this day, in the *Bjeshket shqiptare* (Albanian Alps), one can find rhapsodic singers who praise the deeds of mythical local heroes, or singers who brighten festivals and solemn occasions to the sound of the *lahuta, çifteli* or *sharki*. As Koliqi writes, the arced lifespan of every Albanian is accompanied by the arc of song.

I was always enthralled by the long epic narrations of the Middle Ages, such as the song cycles of Germany and England. In my youth I dreamed of writing long epic poems such as the *Nibelungenlied* or Milton's *Paradise Lost* – or a poem like the Mesopotamian epic of Gilgamesh, the king who, two thousand nine hundred years ago, set out on a quest for life and death. But even more I dreamed of writing an epic poem dedicated to the Albanian leader Scanderbeg. One of the greatest teachings of orality and old lore is that of returning dignity to the word, recovering the epic, musical and civic sense of the word itself, all but lost in contemporary poetry. An alternative to today's stammering poetry. The great epic poets did not use abstractions but tried to express the inner world in precise, concrete sounds and images. Modern European poetry in fact begins with oral epic poetry.

Each one of my collections is a poem reprised in the next collection: my books are nothing but a long, continuous epic poem, and I am a 'singer' whose voice goes out to contemporary man, torn with the wound of being alive and bent under the weight of an old and very sick decadence.

Can you tell me about your contact with the Italian language?

I had a working, or rather, a superficial knowledge of Italian before living in Italy. In Albania I studied Russian and English, since during the Hoxha dictatorship, for ideological reasons, Italian was forbidden as the language of a former Fascist country that had invaded Albania and annexed it to its empire. Albanian schools and universities taught 'patriotic' Italian literature, but a different, clandestine literature circulated alongside official culture. We read forbidden Italian and Latin authors such as Dante, Petrarch, Boccaccio, Ovid, Virgil, Horace, Lucretius, Catullus, and Italian poets branded as decadent such as Ungaretti, Quasimodo, Montale, D'Annunzio, Pascoli. Texts by these authors were secretly copied by hand to escape censorship and the risk of ending up in jail under the charge of 'subversive propaganda against the culture of socialist realism'.

After finding refuge in Italy you began to write in Italian – so your writing unfolds in two languages.

Yes: I write 'in parallel' in both languages, Albanian/Italian and vice versa. It is not a question of bilingualism, but rather of a 'double language'. Both are original languages, so I do not posit 'language' versus 'translation'. Rather than 'translation' I would speak of 'recreation'. I write in Italian and torment myself in Albanian, and vice versa. My migration is not from one country to another, but from one language to the other: this crossing as the poetic experience of language. I work with languages. 'My home-land: my body. / Gëzim: my identity'. In fact, 'Each day in exile I create a new homeland / in which I die and am reborn'. As we know, each writer dialogues with people and worlds by means of language. 'Word' means image, inner self, energy, sacredness. So my writing is a linguistic migra-tion: going in and out, from one language to another, teaching people to be migrants and foreigners. Exile leads to the overcoming of geographical ties and leaves man with no other land than his body. My responsibility, owed to both Albanian and Italian poets, is double.

Most critics call you a 'poet of exile'.

As Eliot said, all poets are exiled, banished from something against their will. The exile is the central image of our century. Since the Temple of the Word was destroyed by 'scribblers', true poets have felt exiled. In any case our land was born in exile. Only an exile can comprehend the world and capture its language, giving a new sense to things, to words. Saints, mys-tics, God himself were exiles, and the history of humanity was always made by exiles. Aspiring writers of today should migrate, so that their Word may confront the love and the wounds of the world. Only the poetry of exiles can leave strong emotions on the memory of Time. I feel very strongly that the beauty of life is not in the living, but in the crossing. 'My country hurts' – as Bresson wrote.

My exile has a thousand eyes, a thousand mouths, a thousand fleeings. In fact I am always fleeing: years ago I fled my country, today in Italy I am in flight each day from the industry of culture, from castrated literature. That's why I am a poet exiled into exile. The exile is a stranger everywhere: firstly in the host country, secondly in his own country, where he no longer feels at home. The only refuge I seek, entrusting it with my word to protect my shaking soul, is writing.

People have commented on your 'monastic demeanour': what is the life story behind it?

'Infandum regina iubes renovare dolorem': O Queen, you ask me to relive an untold sorrow. So Aeneas, answering Dido in Virgil's *Aeneid*: for him, to tell his story means to renew the sorrow of loss, the fall of Troy and the condition of exile. The first person to call me 'the monk of poetry' was my very dear friend Predrag Matvejevic. I strive to be a 'custodian monk' of the Word – only it isn't I who pray in the name of the Word, but the Word that prays in my name. A lay monk who does not try to live life, but to cross it.

My 'habit' hides the story of a child from the outskirts, born and raised on a bleak hill in the province of Darsìa, where in autumn and winter terrible thunderstorms and raging winds hold sway. From the age of ten I had to get up first thing in the morning to take the sheep and goats out to graze; at seven o'clock I would take them back home and then walk to school. My mother would wake me every morning, but sometimes sleep would get hold of me again. It was then that hell would break loose. My father had the herd ready out in the yard and was waiting for me. When he saw that I was still in the house, he would shout out threateningly to my mother: 'Is the cursed one not yet out?' and storm into the one room shared by all of us children. I would jump up as soon as I heard his voice and slip out of the window as he came through the door. 'You will never amount to anything / May you die like a dog!' A curse repeated most days at first light. My solace was my mother. During the day she worked barefoot in the fields of the State Co-operative. In the evening, worn out with exhaustion, she would beg me to take the black thorns from the soles of her feet with a needle. It was she I always asked: 'Why does he always curse me so deeply?' But the worst came if I happened to lose a goat while out grazing: in the evening, there would be no place for me in the house, and I would go to sleep in the hayloft next to my dog. I could hear my mother calling me all through the night, but did not dare go back into the house. I have spoken of this in my collection *Erbamara* (*Bittergrass*), in homage to that little and great daily tragedy in those stern, harsh, but also somehow joyful times.

Albania begets poets. Then she humiliates them, jails, them, rapes their souls, sentences them to silence, tortures them, executes them by firing squad or noose and leaves them unburied, to then save their memory at a later time. Albania is just like Medea devouring her children. The story of

Albanian literature has always been made by the dissident, the exiled, the sentenced, the majority of whom were living abroad. The poets of Tirana only sang for tyrants – in fact my Albania is a country that adores tyrants: I have been invited to read my poetry in several countries worldwide, but not in my Albania, even though I am its main living poet.

I finished secondary and high school in the town of Lushnje; before school, my younger sister and I would sell our milk and yogurt to local families. Each day I walked three hours to go to school and back to the village. During the summer holidays I worked in the fields so as to be able to buy bread and text books. After high school I was accorded the right to attend university. From that time onwards, a real Odyssey of harsh jobs began and continues to this day. I worked for a year as a labourer in land reclamation, then left for military service where I worked with former convicts. I qualified as an accountant in the town of Lushnje and immediately started working in the accounts department of an agricultural Co-operative, a job I held for three years.

At that time I was writing for the most important literary periodicals in Albania. In 1989 I won second prize in the national competition for a best poetry sequence, and my work was published in the weekly *Drita* (*Light*), the journal of the Albanian League Of Writers and Artists. The League intervened on my behalf at government level and I was given the right to attend the Faculty of Letters, with a delay of eight years. I left my job in the accounts department as the co-op would not give me permission to sit university exams. I then found employment as a worker in different factories. One month before the fall of Albanian Stalinism, I was called to the Lyceum and became a teacher there. In that year my collection *Anthology Of Rain* was published, albeit amputated, after five years of rejections.

I was one of the founders of the opposition parties of Lushnje, the Democratic and Republican parties. I was suspended from my teaching post for a week for having taken part, at one o'clock in the morning, in a 'secret' meeting of the opposition. I was elected district secretary of the Albanian Republican Party. In 1992 I ran for the Parliamentary elections, but was defeated by the mafia of the powerful. I denounced the crimes and abuses of both the old Hoxha regime and the new Berisha regime, and for that reason, in 1992, I was forced to leave my country and take refuge in Italy.

For several years I worked various jobs (stables cleaner, hoeman, labourer, assistant typographer), and now live with difficulty on honoraria from conferences and intercultural lectures after obtaining a new degree in Modern Letters at 'La Sapienza' in Rome. I have always earned my bread with my hands – my studies have always somehow caused me trouble. I have never had a bursary, but was always a working student and never could attend lectures.

What is poetry for you?

For me poetry is, first and foremost, Life – and life means engagement: the writer cannot run from life and from History. A real writer is always in conflict with the conventions of his time. This is a great European tradition, from Dante to Brecht, from Pasolini to Sartre; but also Neruda, Majakovskij, Hugo, Ritsos, Leopardi, Paz, Borges even, Walcott, Senghor, Trebeshina, Mandelstam, Blok, Gumiljev, Brodskij, Achmatova, Tsvetaeva, Hikmet, Aragon, Bellezza, Machado, Quasimodo, the Beat Generation, Whitman, Enzensberger, De Moraes, Rushdie and others have lived inside the human sorrow of their times. Most of these poets were condemned together with their work. They were tortured, deported, driven insane, banished from their countries or brutally murdered because they were engaged in the struggle for freedom against injustice and corruption, fundamentalism and crimes against humanity.

If we go back to the history of ancient Greece, we can see how Sophocles was a good citizen, engaged, twice a strategist for Athens and one of the six magistrates who drafted the constitution of the city-state. In archaic Greece, the man of letters would sing to the events, as it were, whereas in the classical period he would always address the people, considering himself a spokesman for the community, charged with a civil and pedagogical mission on behalf of the citizens who were in direct relationship with him: they were at the same time his audience, his judges and his patrons. In Rome, the man of letters performs a public function in his capacity as *cives romanus*. Because each work of literature is first and foremost a moral act: it can save and change lives. The more contemporary man accumulates on the outside, the more beggarly and barren he grows inside. Poetry helps us survive, teaches us about beauty and ugliness, love and hate, war and peace; it shakes up consciousness, creates alternative worlds.

The hermeneutics of Heidegger and Gadamer, of Derrida and Steiner, have taught us to read a work of art as the herald of a world in which we must learn to live, rather than an object that we can place alongside others on a shelf. Poetry also is engagement – not only with the verse or the language, as some 'great' contemporary men of letters would have us believe, but with Life.

Belinda Cooke

Days of the Shorthanded Shovelists: The Irish Come to London.

Tim Pat Coogan in *Wherever Green is Worn: the Story of the Irish Diaspora* (Arrow Books, 2002) gives a gruelling picture of what conditions were like for Irish workers coming to London in the fifties – around 20,000 a year, here paraphrasing a social worker's report of the time:

> a house in which Fifty young Irishmen lived, paying a rent of £2 a week each for the privilege of sleeping 15 to a room, and supplying and cooking their own food. It was commonplace in such accommodation for male shift workers to occupy the beds by day, and girls to do so by night. The sanitary conditions were often 'appalling', and the diet of these unfortunates, most of whom had no idea of how to cook, consisted of little more than tea and buns. Needless to say, there was a high incidence of alcholism, TB, and gastroenteritis, amongst the Irish population.
>
> (p. 162)

Speaking as one whose parents came out of that economic migration, to me Coogan's book was a revelation, particularly when I saw the photo of two young Irish girls, in their best dress (didn't all our parents before the invention of the teenager dress like that?) arriving at an English train station. These girls were my mother. She came over to Camden and worked in a hotel for little more than 'a roof over you head' as she told me. Perhaps, it's a sign of ageing when you see yourself as part of history, as a type.

Yet this was also the period that was going to lead into the sixties boom time and many of those Irish came and made money. Our generation were to reap the rewards of their hardships. But the second revelation for me came with the appearance of Jon McGregor's 'A Long Way Back' (*The Guardian Weekend* 30 April 2011) which reviews the film documentary *Arise You Gallant Sweeneys* (outsidefilm@mail.com) about the numerous Irish male workers who simply worked and drank and could never even get the fare to go back home:

> They tell me about cooking breakfast on a shovel on the building sites (the trick apparently, being to wedge a couple of mushrooms

either side of the sausages to keep them from rolling off), about men being conned into selling their national insurance numbers, about being paid in the pub and finding work in the pub, and borrowing money in the pub that kept them tied to the gangerman until the following week's payday. 'If you didn't drink, you weren't wanted', Sean says. 'You were an outcast'.

(p. 41)

My childhood has many memories of such characters and the cynic in me doesn't recall anyone's arm being twisted to make the pub venue, yet looking back now with a more sociological eye, such men were very much victims of their time. Mcgregor's article also reveals the other key characteristic (which led Virginia Woolf to make the comment that Ireland is full of poets), that pseudo-philosophical-humorous trait reminiscent of Sean O'Casey's *Juno and the Paycock* expressed in one of the men's response as to why they came in the first place: 'Why does a man go anywhere?... He's got to go somewhere. What's the difference? He's got to live somewhere!'

My father worked on the buildings all his life. He liked his drink and his dogs and horses but he was one who would be considered to have made it – the ganger giving out the subs. Yet he, like his brother, was also a victim of this less health-conscious age, dying in his early fifties from a work-related incident when a pipe ricocheted into his eye because he wasn't wearing safety goggles. His brother who came to London with him fell from scaffolding a few years later and he wasn't wearing a safety helmet. Memories of my father are also wrapped in endless examples of this mock-intellectual wit of his less driven compatriots. To name but one: when I asked him what I should say at school in response to the question what he did for a living: 'Just tell them I'm a short-handed shovelist'.

This selection of poems touches on the economic pressures the working Irish experienced in the decades preceding my parents' generation and through to the sixties boom time.

Hunger

They never spoke about it
only they did say
(yes I think they said
something) about the
grave of a child
somewhere
near the house –
they did say that.

Giving Delia the Ring

How could it have happened
in that day and age
with a man who didn't drink,
and owned his own radio?

They gave you to her
because we were so many and
sure she had no one
and you were one to envy
with the best of everything
while we were left to struggle.

But when everyone went to England
you'd wander down the empty house
run about the barn
look through the window
and imagine playing with all of us there
like your secret friends.

So when mammy died
we gave you her ring
though Anne was less than pleased
as you can imagine.

The *Craic*

When Nixon was being forced into a corner
language was evolving on the building sites:
'We'll have to impeach that one… he's no use at all.'

For years I heard my father talk
of his mysterious co-workers:
'Shtiff' the man in charge of the mixer,
'the ex-cre*hh*mery manager' – for his past status.

Or those men in the backroom bars on the journey west:
'Shakespeare came here once you know...
he said they were the best days of his life.'

Me, mooning over the local heartbreaker
son of a country man turned townie
with an ice cream shop to free himself from the soil

Sub

You'd give him the half crown
just by way of 'an entrance fee',
then the lads would keep him in drink
for the rest of the session.

Days of the Short-Handed Shovelists

They'd lean on their shovels
waiting for the stiff rake of concrete
dressed in their third best suits
grit and nails in the pockets,
the pavement's patchwork tarmac
melting and soft in the mid-summer heat,
unbearable aroma you could eat –
street charmers giving women the glad eye
in between the loads of concrete.
You could do this, the best of the rest,
only to end in a ricocheted pipe
that happened so easy using the wrong tool,
and Jim with no helmet
as he fell from the scaffolding.
Copycat deaths: slow tick
of the life support machine
till we decide to switch it off
accepting it won't change anything.

Dreaming of *Blue Peter* Mothers

Not enough to lick the bowl,
I needed a *Fairy Liquid* sewing box,
and peppermint iced-sweets…
Where were you when I needed you
to catch that fleeting address?

Stuck with that hand wringer,
pleading with me – to be 'good' for the day:
bare feet sulking in the washing scum,
wrists indelible mauve ink twigs,
infinite 'me's in the three-tiered mirror.

My dolls all had grotesque stuck eyes
and plastic fingers hard to chew:
I'd strip them naked, force them to
unmentionable acts of humiliation –
to midnight wasps and barbed wire sheets.

Greg Delanty

To Those Who Stayed

Brand us *exiles, emigrants* if you like.
It may make your life easier, may buttress
You, shield you, maybe even help hike
Your spirits up, help you feel superior to us.

You will need it as you traverse streets
That you brag you can walk blindfold on.
But where's that shop, that bar? No one greets
You any more; so many are dead, or, like us, gone.

Perhaps we were shrewder, wiser, more cunning.
Perhaps not. What's certain is that more
And more your city is abandoning you, forgetting
You, as if the city itself is crossing to another shore,

Leaving you nothing and no one, an immigrant
In your own place, the oblivious emigrant.

David Cooke

Going Home

Stage Irish, for sure, and patriotic to a fault,
you were self-styled *Irish John,*
defining yourself by allegiance

to a place that doesn't exist
beyond exiled memories.
Through intransigent years

of bomb blasts, reprisals,
you picked over endlessly
the bleak bones of history

with me goading you
to tell me why you never returned,
knowing contentiousness

was your delight, the devilment,
in a schoolboy
who winked each time

they caned him. Fearless
to the end, you were ready to go,
and so I'll say goodbye,

trying now to get it right –
how one who leaves says *slán agat!*
and one who remains *slán leat!*

Gerard Smyth

It was Autumn but he called it *The Fall*

It was autumn but he called it 'The Fall'.
The American uncle, home with his dollars
to the land of shillings and pence;
home with a twang in his voice
that made him sound like Eastwood in *Rawhide*.

He had come back after years,
his sojourn lasted weeks;
memories were the treasury he carried –
of the emigrant ship, the shore-to-shore Atlantic;
his first sight of an horizon

that was a latticework of fire escapes,
of buildings configured to hide the sky.
Home at last, he went looking for turf stacks
long turned to smoke and ash,
failed to recognise the woman who was a child

when he departed with his only inheritance,
the Brigid's Cross placed in his hands,
the one-way ticket to different pastures –
New York in its jazz age,
where a shy Hibernian boy hadn't the courage to dance.

Liam O'Muírthile

Cumannach

Bhraitheas dáimh lena ghiall
cearnógach, lena chaint righin,
is snoíodh a chloigeann as bloc
sa chairéal gur gearradh cloch
as do mhúnla m'uncailí féin.
Chuirfidís siúd cos i bhfeac
ag sluaisteáil ar feadh a saoil
i monarcha siúcra, ar fheirm tobac,
nó chaitheadar uathu é sa tsioc
mar obair shalach i muileann lín,
Is thugadar a n-aghaidh soir siar
ar Bhirmingham, Chicago, Perth,
is cailíní na Carraige ina ndiaidh
ag déanamh cosán dearg amach
as tír na bhfead glaice nach raibh faic
Ann ach gaoth an mhacalla
is bheith sásta le géillsine thoil Dé
fé mar a bheadh sé féin toilteanach
éisteacht leis an gcoileach ag fógairt
an lae bhréagaigh, amhscarnach baoth.
Sheas sé leis an mbocht go docht
is má bé a locht a laghad a bhí sé
sásta bogadh ó sheasamh an Chreimlín,
baineann dínit le dorn ar an stiúir
daingean, duineanda go tóin poill.

Communist

I felt drawn to his
square jaw, tough talk,
head cut from a quarry
block, the very same
as my own uncles' mould.
They knew how to dig in,
shovelling all their lives
in a sugar factory, on a tobacco farm,
or throwing it all to the winds –
filthy work in the flax mills,
Heading east, west,
to Birmingham, Chicago, Perth,
and the Ballinacarriga girls after them
beating tracks away
from the land of wolf whistles
with nothing there for them but spectres
of an echo
Telling them to be happy vassals of God's will,
as though he himself would dare
to listen to the cock announcing
a false dawn, another fool's day.
He stood firmly by the poor
and though his fault was ever
to hold course to the Kremlin,
there's dignity in going down
undaunted, as a man, with the ship.

Peter Dale

The Hurlers

I cannot answer your decree, outlanders.
I do not jaw the jargon that you bark.
You perpetrate such howlers, alien blunders.
My speech is not according to your book.

I know your euphemisms through loud-hailers
In every would-be rule you up and utter.
Try speaking to the moors, command The Hurlers.
We hold the inward; they the granite outer.

Our language, our culture, raised that monument
And thousands like it; only in foolish legends
Can they be moved – by night and devilish command,
Steadfast strong-holders, unbudged by legions.

Our tongue is whispering. Hark, a knifing draught.
Our megaliths mark your star-fall. You're cast adrift.

Note: The Hurlers are three Bronze Age stone circles near the famous Cheese Wring
Megaliths. Somewhat damaged and ruinous, they are still impressive, although their
name is less so, based on a mediaeval Christian legend that they represent teams of
men petrified for the sin of playing the Celtic game of hurling on the Sabbath.

Grey Gowrie

Black Trout: Reading 1948

How odd, how consolingly weird,
that a writer seeking an image for his love
chose a black trout, in the river Thames, at Reading:
polluted town of gravel and biscuitry.
Ancient bream or predatory pike
perhaps; seldom that lithe elated flail.

After the war, in bankrupt utilitarian
England the boy lived a few miles downstream
at Windsor. The King used to come to tea
with anxious protuberant eyes and controlled stammer.
At ease with children, he told his equerry
to slip him a shilling. Sweets were still 'on the ration'.
Major Thing had half-a-crown only – more than double –
and whispered that he was doing well.
                    The Governor, a VC,
and His Majesty took a turn round the Moat Garden
with pipe and gasper, to give privy counsel and get it.

If only, *maestro*, you had rented a car,
driven a few miles south, to Stratfield Saye, say,
and the Loddon, or a few miles further, and the Test,
retired officers, some quite badly wounded,
would have kitted you out for the piscatorial
challenge of all time: stalking a pound-and-a-half
wild brown trout with red iridescent markings
and silver belly: an individual you spotted
hours before and among long wavering grasses
and treacherous cast-catching willows floated your false
irrelevant insect, more nuisance than food,
from a waxed line to dance less than an inch
in front of his sneering mouth; then judged the second
between his taking it in and spitting it out
to strike with your Hardy, strike, but not too hard.

You would have earned your metaphor, your tight lines
to win that far-off, faintly identified
woman and ease her into the open creel
of your heart.

     The Test, *padrone*, not the Thames.
Clear waters well from chalk, not muddy clay
as the boy knew, and might have taken you in hand.

Argyll Tour: Glasgow 1948

Rich and poor circle
the ship-building city
like gulls who feed
off anything; cigarette
butts; toffee paper; even,
it's said, the eyes of sheep
driven down hills to queue
in front of an abattoir.
Your Clyde sweats
oil and tar...

For a few pounds, you cover
a frenzy of islands; for a few more,
hire your own man to show you
harbour life.
          It rains a lot but the sun shines
more than they say. You know the city
is only a boat, after all; a tributary
of the Irish Sea, small sliver of the Atlantic.

Where, you ask yourself, am I going
and what can I be doing? Ossian
never spoke well to you and you never visited
Fingal's Cave on Staffa, the great Turner
in the Brooklyn Museum. America
beckons; an unbroken horse
lashes out in his pen and splinters
what's left of your heart.
             The stable mice
find you ridiculous. Sleek liners
built in this town will carry you over the water
whenever you summon the nerve to board them.
Years later, thinking about you, I know you won't.

By coincidence we find ourselves in the same
quarter of vanished time. It is 1948.
I am eight years old, you around fifty:
timid, lovelorn, indecisive, a giant of letters.

My family want me to visit Great Uncle Hugo,
dying and still quite rich from ship broking.
I have nothing to say. He grunts and dribbles
and needs to be fed.
                    From my bedroom window
I watch seals on the beach flex their moustaches.
Weak sunsets illumine the Paps of Jura.
I long to be back on the night train from Glasgow,
comforted by the little electric blue
nightlight above my bunk on the Euston sleeper,
the rails' monotonous grind. Going home.
                              You, all over the place,
try to anchor yourself with a catalogue
of urban impressions: the canals; the ragamuffins;
clatter of chains as the boats cast off;
the mildewy, mushroomy smell when a squall passes;
a vagrant's laugh or cry and everywhere
shadows of gulls with their intermittent screaming,
the song that money sings, and no money.
                              At ten o'clock
lights come on, gulls start to disappear,
quills of smoke rise from rationed coal.
It won't wash. You know perfectly well
you need a name and the face and the body
                              to put to that name,
emerge through the foreign gloom and try to enslave you.

Josephine Balmer

Agricola's Retirement

...it was generally believed that the province of Britain
would be his, not because he had lobbied for it but because
he was deemed worthy of it...

Tacitus, *Agricola*, 9

He was asking the wrong questions,
my son-in-law, Rome's great historian,
as he measured out lines or balanced
tactics, reducing our lives to raw syntax.
But most of all I needed to tell Tacitus
how it felt to have reached so far, the furthest

north any Roman had ever come; of a June
afternoon in Britain I buried a son, Thule
faint as a faded promise on the horizon,
knowing I would never return to mourn him.
Then I went out to battle, to breed that same grief:
they create a wasteland and call it peace...

Afterwards I walked in those northern forests,
their unearthly twilight seeping on past sunset;
the hacked limbs, the mounds of the fallen,
skies soaking up spilt blood like a sponge.
I had stepped off the edge of the known
world and was standing in the meadows

of the faded stars; on grass flayed by the breeze,
caught in the nets of skeletal wildflower seed;
clouds spiralled above like shattered sphincters,
linking us together, conquered and conqueror.
The furthest any Roman had ever come.
The living and the dead in a moth's wingspan.

I knew then we would see our sons again.

Note: According to his son-in-law, the Roman historian Tacitus, Agricola was
governor of Britain from AD 77-85, during which time he mounted a campaign
to subdue northern Scotland. Tacitus claimed that Agricola won a great victory
at 'Mons Graupius', thought to be the Grampian mountains, and also mentions
'Ultima Thule', a Latin name for any distant region beyond the known world, here
thought to refer to Orkney. Whatever the success of Agricola's campaigns, the
Romans withdrew and did not attempt a conquest of the Highlands again.

Cavafy's Things

(*after* The Afternoon Sun)

We knew it at once: the faded grooves
touched by the afternoon sun.
The crack where we'd left it too long
in the window, splitting the wood in two.
The candle wax we'd scrubbed but not removed.

Ah, yes, this table, it was our family.

We'd seen it last in the collection van,
shrouded by its matching chairs.
Now here it was in the newly-opened cafe
(had it been an office for commercial affairs?
Or maybe a solicitor's? No, the baker's...),
lined round in pine, tarnished, second-hand;
a resting-place for dust-caked builders
slumped over strong tea, the full English,
as dark and heady as funeral incense.

They must always have been around somewhere,
those worn-out old things...

On the other side, the place where she laughed
every birthday, all those festive lunches;
in the centre, the faint circle of a wine glass
set down to carry in warmed plates or dishes,
indelible now, an ever-bleeding blemish.

That afternoon, at 4 o'clock, we said goodbye
for one week only... I thought I'd see her.
And then that week became forever.

Robert Smith

Sveta

The taste of
black bread in her voice,
émigré singer

under the larches
of a Berlin garden
in the twenties,

drawing dustsheets
over furniture, leaving
her dolls to starve,

orchards to the axe,
the timetabling of railways
turned over to servants,

and a pose held tirelessly,
moulding herself to a lineage
of lost cadences:

poured out on 78s,
even the trees are weeping
her tears of static.

Omar Sabbagh

Hearty Quiet

For Mohamad Sabbagh

Frightening to think the lay of day may die,
Like a poem made suddenly boneless, like a snake,
Too lardy a fit for the ashy ground, too quiet

For humdrum sibilance, the charged hiss of *'why'*?
One day, a man may dance, another, pond-calm, and like a lake –
Frightening to think the lay of day may die.

And if there's love in a basket of berries, twice
The red of red, let all the grays be brittle and break –
I, too fat a fit for the ashy ground, simply: too quiet;

As though death were a She, silence nuanced, and nice
Among varied digits, fingers, what the wailing knuckles wake
By way of moving fear: to think the lay of day may die.

The glass of my insides shatters, or becomes like sodden rice,
Slantwise, in some Asian field, where it rains so hard, it's hate,
A hate too fat for the ashy ground, white-hot, say, and quiet.

There's only one villain within this tale, though a choir's choice,
As minstrels move to a sudden sadness: fools become rakes –
O! It's frightening to think the lay of day may die:
A mundane father turned to smoke, voice of oak: hearty quiet.

Martyn Crucefix

Son to father

Past ninety and still no books to read . . .
Your knuckles rapping at the meal table

gestures alongside a stumbling of words
so much aware of their inadequacy

it hurts us both but in different ways
since a man without language is no man –

too late to discover the absence of words
has built a prison, you're no longer able

to dominate objects as once you did
the world revolving in your loosening grip.

Sudeep Sen

Kargil

Our street of smoke and fences, gutters gorged
with weed and reeking, scorching iron grooves
of rusted galvanise, a dialect forged
from burning asphalt, and a sky that moves
with thunderhead cumuli grumbling with rain, ….
                    Derek Walcott, *Tiepolo's Hound*

Ten years on, I came searching for
war signs of the past
expecting remnants – magazine debris,
unexploded shells,
shrapnels
that mark bomb wounds.

I came looking for
ghosts –
people past, skeletons charred,
abandoned
brick-wood-cement
that once housed them.

I could only find whispers –
whispers among the clamour
of a small town outpost
in full throttle –
everyday chores
sketching outward signs
of normalcy and life.

In that bustle
I spot war-lines of a decade ago –
though the storylines
are kept buried, wrapped
in old newsprint.

There is order amid uneasiness –
the muezzin's cry,
the monk's chant –
baritones
merging in their separateness.

At the bus station
black coughs of exhaust
smoke-screens everything.
                          The roads meet
and after the crossroad ritual
diverge,
skating along the undotted lines
of control.
A porous garland
with cracked beads
adorns Tiger Hill.
Beyond the mountains
are dark memories,
and beyond them
no one knows,
and beyond them
no one wants to know.

Even the flight of birds
that wing over their crests
don't know which feathers to down.
Chameleon-like
they fly,   tracing perfect parabolas.

I look up
and calculate their exact arc
and find instead,   a flawed theorem.

Caroline Clark

Olkhon, Baikal,

where the girl by the well
thought she'd turned foreign
by talking to me. Full

with her sudden talent:
I speak English well. Yes,
you do, and now let me

look at you a while. Fog
from the forest fires, we
never saw across your famed

lake to the Shaman's headland.
Your cheekbones spoke of steppe.
The sun, a veiled lamp coming on,

off, on. Cold was the summer.
And into the interior we headed.
Look back – the fog, look front.

Foreign is all I know. You
take my language, travel
on it, sell it, go far, then

come back home unable ever
to stay in one place again.

New City

Every place you aren't
reminds us where we're not.
A waterfall thundering past
the vertical black of night.
Day brings an advance:
your kids will like it here.

Inside I look out through
the winter undergrowth
to trains going by.
Metal, gold, silver, red,
ten Canada minutes' long
and I'm gone to that place
glimpsed in a meltwater puddle.
Clear water. Sunlit sand.
See-through to the other side.

It's like looking at that moon
last night. Over the shoulder
smile to say
what I knew would be there
was.

John Griffin

Monk's Elm

Do you recall the spaces opened by the sun in the shadows
of youth, infancy's tongue tongue-tied by waves of wrath,
the muslin curtains, the dust and the chimes and sometimes cries
from the darkness at the center of a scene, a cut-out scene,
punched through a hole in memory and shaped to fit everywhere
except where it most belonged in your heart of hours?
Do you recall the black puddle in your path you could not cross?
Your whole world became unreal to you and, suspended at its core
without co-ordinates, you bore in your arms your naked, infant life,
and you took up residence in absence there and dipped your hands
in the blood of light to finger-paint your past anew:
This was the room you knew, your own room, smelling of sour milk
and fat, with shadows off their head and the empty spaces
whispering of dead kings and cruelty's wings and voyages out
into the unsaid tides, steered by silence, with presumption's jetty
racing to embrace you into sanctum's shore. Awake now
among the hills and the spring fields, with not a current in sight,
but a sea's rhythm in your veins and an Ophelia invocation rippling
on every stream, you waded out to where your center rose
restored at last and then you sank into the inky well of yourself.

Jeremy Page

A Different Account

I don't know who
wrote these letters
recording every detail
of my student life
and wanderings round
the London postcodes.
Memory tells a different story
from these pages, where
I never spend a lonely night
and poverty's a ball.

The hand could be mine
and the addresses are familiar,
but the style's the style
of someone I no longer know
as if I've come in
half-way through a novel,
so the characters are
no more than names,
the plot so Chandleresque,
it can't be fathomed.

If I'd died and you'd lived,
your letters to me returned,
would you recognise yourself
in them at sixteen, twenty, thirty?
Was I ever the person
you thought you knew?
And who was it
I really wrote to?

Merryn McCarthy

Crossing Over

Road take us there,
the river yielding,
ferry waiting, a full tide.

Wish tree and dancing tree
left to their rhythms.
In the ship's wake

we are unleashed –
the white cliffs
fall behind.

A grey sea heaves
in our hearts –
all we have known.

No right of return.
Landfall assumes
an uncertain light.

Marek Urbanowicz

River Meeting

He has been mired here a long time
on this dark side of the river
waiting for her sure arrival
to this ghosted, estranging place
with felled angels, strangers, paled shades,
where the air is fetid and dank,
where the wind makes no scything sound,
has no cardinals, where water
does not mirror and actions
carry no refractive ripple.

Knowing he can't be ferried back,
or swim the black waters to be
beached with the penniless who pine
a hundred years to then be poled
across the sorrowful river,
– with its mists, deceiving currents –
he bides his slowed time, or rather
he is bidden to wait, un-sensed,
stripped bare of touch or of keening.

He has known forced exile, a kind
of dying from his former life,
still nurturing the hope that once
the iron curtain has rusted,
he'll return. This was different,
slow purgation loosens his soul,
he has made peace with the two wives
who bore his children, his anger.

Would she be as he remembered
intelligent, bespectacled,
nervously determined, English.
And would his feelings be the same,
had he been eviscerated
of all those old emotions,
blooded of his bile and humours?

Then the creak of oars, the dull ring
of the obolus in the mouth
of Charon the boatman's pocket,
and her, diaphanous and pale,
calling him as she used to do,
naming him with her innocence.

And she was as he recalled her,
a bright-eyed, kindly soul who had
unruffled him, unstitched his pains,
healed, in those last years, the fracture,
taken the exile from his eyes.

Their twinned voices drifted, away
from the river, leaving behind
the ferryman and their past lives
like cast offs on the other side,

and ghosted over the meadows,
the hosts of yellow asphodel,
to arrive at this new river

where they bathed their feet and forgot,
and, in the forgetting, became

twined hovers of smoke on Lethe.

Deborah Moffatt

Eating Thistles

We ate thistles, and spoke a language
as sharp and barbed as the wire on their walls.

We slept on stone, bathed in snow,
made combs from thorns, clothes from nettles.

Words froze on our tongues
and fell in frozen lumps on barren land.

In their cities and in their towns
they gloried in victory, a nation once again.

We heard their pipes and their drums,
gunshot, fireworks, songs of celebration.

Maddened by power, powered by madness,
they closed their borders, then turned against their own.

Better to sleep on stone, however hard;
better to eat thistles, though we choke;

better our frozen silence than their fiery rhetoric;
better thorns and nettles than pomp and glory;

better to die in a barren wilderness
than to survive in a nation born of vanity.

W S Milne

Fremmit

Hurryin here and there, warslin aawey,
Stravaigin ower the waves – ti whaur?
Anither ploos the laund wi new gear –
Aa the skeels o the smith and builder,
Clerk and writer,
Hired for their wisdom, their knack o trade,
This ain skeeled in peace, this ain in war –
Doctors, professors, teachers aa –
Haddin aff the derkness and pain.
At nicht they dream o their mither's haunds
And o faces o their lang-gaan hame.

Note:

Fremmit: stateless, friendless; *warslin:* wrestling; *aawey:* everywhere;
stravaigin: labouring; *whaur:* where; *ploos:* ploughs; *skeels:* skills;
haddin: holding; *derkness:* darkness

Rosalind Hudis

House Clearance

After forty years in the same plot,
turned East, by a window, soaking
the moments when someone unloads,

sloughs off their shoes,
my mother's sofa is planted
outside on the lawn. Its soft

caramel hide would blister
in the climate of a garden life,
the plunge to frost,

the unlidded night,
city foxes wicking
carnal plastic from bins.

When my just widowed mother sits
down there as she always sits,
memorial and still, I think the sun

will not be kind to her skin,
its lines of blurred ink, like a letter kept
too long, won't read

their way correctly along the paths.
Behind her, golden rod and cosmos
plait and unplait the sky

and it's not the gape of something
caught rootless, in her face, but the sly
dawn delirium of free.

Sheenagh Pugh

The Edges

He hangs around the edges
where things happen,

the shoreline where land is eaten
and shells wash up

empty. Where countries stop
midstream, or at barbed wire

and rifle posts. Where walls meet air
at windowsills, balconies, parapets.

Most often, though, he waits
on time's borders, the rim

where light and dark bleed, become
other, the red pen-stroke

that is Walker, his mark,
the end of days.

Nausheen Eusuf

Elegy for My Nephew and Niece

Tempe, Arizona

Soon I learn to decode their excited chatter:
the science project, the henhouse chronicles,
soccer, swimming, learning Arabic on Sundays,
the time she got sick, the time he fell off his bike,
their lives laid open with marvellous unreserve.

Then it's show and tell: a trove of foreign coins,
batteries, marbles, paper clips in animal shapes,
a pair of dice, debris from a dismembered watch,
a pebble, a seashell, an odd piece from a puzzle,
a golden penny discovered in the grass.

Unfazed by the desert sun, they rush out to play
with the chickens and inspect the nest box for eggs.
Seemingly tireless, their small bodies, lean and lithe,
bound over flower beds and compost heaps, checked
only by the day's gradual dissolution into dusk.

In the evening, they sit hunched over a jigsaw
puzzle, fitting piece after painstaking piece.
Contours emerge – the arm of a saguaro,
a flower-like ocotillo, an endless sandscape,
a sunset leaking its radiance across the sky.

If only this could always be. If only they could
never grow up, never grow old, never to vanish
traceless into the eternity of sand and sun
that leaves nothing but the towering saguaro
reaching towards the fierce blue of a Sonoran sky.

Where We Do Not Think To Think

I am not wherever I am the plaything of my thought;
I think of what I am where I do not think to think.
                                        – Jacques Lacan

The more we think, the less we know and the deeper sink
in the quicksand of words our fathers unthinking wrought.
We think of what we are where we do not think to think.

Only once were we ourselves and all the world in sync:
before the mirror and the fall, we knew ourselves untaught.
The more we think, the less we know and the deeper sink

in desire's dismal abyss. What we lost and lack, no shrink
can cure; nor fancy's wing deliver us from the snare of thought
to where we simply are, where we do not think to think.

We think before and after, yet each thought is but a link
in the great chain that holds us bound and bought.
The more we think, the less we know and the deeper sink

in a conjured world where things vanish with a wink,
elusive and sublime, and all our longings come to naught.
We think of what we are where we do not think to think,

where signs dissolve like the careful cursive penned in ink
now faded by lovers long ago whom once we sought.
The more we think, the less we know and deeper sink;
we think of what we are where we do not think to think.

Maria Taylor

Yiayia's House

Nothing more than two rooms
painted white, with a smell of wheat
around the bedding. On hot nights
we'd sit on her old woven chairs
just talking, very nearly asleep.

Through an insistent *jurr jurr*
of crickets, Yiayia's voice was soft.
She'd bless her dead husband,
my grandfather, who was wise
and kept an electric light outside
the house, so that insects flew
around the bulb's queenly moon
with their fast wings learning
how to whisper in her presence.

Note:

Yiayia is a Greek word, often used by children, for grandmother. My own
grandmother wasn't an immigrant, but my father was. We went on a family holiday
when I was a child, which would have been his first time back after twenty five
years. As a child I was struck by the way the family seemed to revolve around my
grandmother; she seemed to be at the centre of everything.

William Bedford

The Potato Gatherers

for my father

The potato gatherers were the ones,
Van Gogh faces in a Van Gogh barn,
where they slept upstairs after work,
or rested when they weren't working.
'They're counting the harvest',
your sister reckoned. 'Or maybe praying'.
You thought they were witches,
chanting to fetch curses from the dark.

The Methodist minister said the same:
'Decent folk don't pray on their knees,
or out of doors, like cattle.'
From Manchester himself,
he often talked of cattle,
as though the farmers in the pews
would understand his parables better
if he used the language of herds.

The hens got mithered either way,
quacking at whoever stole their eggs
for the field workers' breakfasts.
In a lane, you found a string of beads
and took them to the minister.
He pronounced them a curse
that would bring famine and pestilence,
panic among the young women.

Nothing much happened.
The potato gatherers went home
when the potato harvest was finished.
The minister was driven away by an aunt
who said she'd seen all this before,
he wasn't a man made for loneliness.
The blacksmith put a new lock on the barn,
and the fields sank back into silence.

You walked with your sister to chapel,
harvest supper and then a dance.
You didn't care for dancing. In a corner,
you ran the string of beads
between your fingers,
and they chattered like pebbles in the beck,
or the crows when you went crow-scaring,
humming a music nobody recognised.

Nigel Jarrett

Axeman

That monster looming out of the night
is next door's cruciform willow. I think
Bert has overdone it this time, but assures
us that it will come again, like the Jesus Christ
he's always appealing to when, aloft
with that tool he says was made for the job,
his footing gives and he splits a finger.
At night he's like the Holy Son himself,
his flurry of wounds by jab and prick
dulled as he weaves his way home
from the Crown, dropping to his knees
now and again in benedictive mode.

But he'll be risen by six the next morning
and fighting the good fight in an hour,
the grub-like mattress mould dissolving
as surely as his knobbly creations will again
shake their spears at him, given a winter to re-group.

Persephone

She was ever the sober one, fleeing
the shadow of his late 'difficulty'
on days out with her gang
and returning with one more exotic
for her festoon of prizes from beyond
the borders. Hidden among them now
their Pre-Cambrian joint purchases:
the stone cat from Appleby; the thyme
pinched by an Orton seedsman in Castellina;
that reluctant dwarf olive from Lydney.

The 'pathetic phallus' joke she coined
reminds him of her now. He weeds religiously,
ticking the timetable over half-moons.
Cystus flowers on the lash stare glassy-eyed
before falling over at midnight in a heap.
And there's that high-ground guardian,
old jasmine, its perfume a spectre's presence.

Mary Fitzpatrick

Refugees

There goes the dream and its
  inhabitants, fleeing
   in their tiny cart, all
    belongings piled high, a
     colored rug, a hookah,
     samovar, the baby
      solemn-faced as a judge –
      fleeing too, the wizened
      donkey, its tiny hooves
       pinging the cobblestones
       up and over the hill
        gloomy in sulphur light
        for this, after all, is
         war – or perhaps it's a
        ruin of crops and soil –
       and the bearded man knows
      this is the final time
     he will see his city,
     his gaze a handkerchief
    settling on each building,
    and he guessed it would pass
   this way, yet she, chilled in
   her mother-woven shawl,
  promises return, her
 heart a witness, the child
 beside her who, to be
real, must have a country
since memory comes from place,
that clod of earth in our shoes.

Stephen Yeo

(From A China Scrapbook)

For whom is now a better time than then?

i

For the peasant who took his tortoise
one thousand kilometres from home,
to Dong Hu Lake in Hubei province:

the lake feeds into the Yangtze;
he put the tortoise in (as is the custom)
to home, like a pigeon.

Twenty-six years later,
the tortoise came home.
'This is his best so far', the peasant said,

'but he can do better.
Next time he comes home,

I shall be dead'.

ii

For the Kuomintang veteran from Sichuan
exiled to Taiwan in nineteen forty-nine,
a lifetime later, back on the Yangtze.

Up river in Sichuan, he found no home:
drowned; too near the flood line.
His dead brother's son-in-law received him.

Down river from Hubei province to Shanghai,
on one last journey through the Gorges,
the old soldier said –

should his first wife not be found there –
'I shall look in Manchuria,
for that was where she came from'.

Ruth O'Callaghan

The Silence Unheard

We had heard the three notes of the dove and seen
the curve of light against a naive sky, had smelt

unguent from crushed palms beneath our feet
and were caught between hosanna and crucifixion.

Knowing what was written we were afraid
of what may be demanded, wary of that we may discover

beyond birth. So, yes, we did travel slowly, each decision
an indecision, each suggestion once, twice, questioned

but at the first snow-melt we began our journey,
followed rivers in full flood from the abundance that ice

had borne through winter's keep, had, at the hint
of a reluctant spring, chosen, if choice were possible,

release. Of course, dying framed the silence.
There was the call of one reaching out for the comforting

cry of another, the hand held, a touch,
though all were beyond the reach of language, beyond

those small hypocrisies of death. The first true birth.
The knot cut close.

For what is the past but the scar of other centuries, a spike
of time to beat against locked doors? And who will dare

to open to the stranger whose words are differently chosen,
whose promise is release? Yet, unhope,

framing the silence, clings tight as a caul and krumholz
smothers abandoned gardens

where those who have sown thought falter. Perhaps,
only the blind man, he who rocks at the edge of the known,

his world a long cane's length, may pierce those dark tangles,
may witness what is written.

But who would believe in the word of the unseeing?
Or know in the unseen is the silence unheard?

Yet when the bleed of shadow behind the sun
darkened the sky

we held fast to the charred end of that day,
knew the cry was the pith reluctant to release the flesh.

And still we failed, unprepared
for linen unwound, the re-composition, sheltered by stone.

Stuart Medland

Coast to Coast

You saw me off.

Drove me to Sunderland, the
Bike on the roof in the rain – saddle
Wrapped in a polythene bag.

There was no-one here this early on so damp
A Wearside day. I could safely dip a trainer
In the Sea. Then Coast to Coast it was.

You hardly knew how you might say Goodbye to me.

Time and again along the dockland cycle path
I risked a clattering against the railings,
Looking back to see you, standing,
Smaller, and still rainier without a coat,
There, by the car.

Watching me cycle
Out of our lives.

Dear Aunty Joyce

It is a Judas and ichneumon love
That gives you leave to simply melt away.

All filigree connections between
                    loves and times and places
Fizzle to a stub
Inside your head; a head that
Recognises everybody
As a turnip. Every
Neuron fattened on a
Sunday afternoon and
Bundled up, with others, into
Happy consciousness,
Dissolved, like
Parasitised inchworms,
From the inside out.

Swollen into some root vegetable, yourself,
Plonked into a soil, hosed
With water when they
Changed the bedclothes.

At what point did you have no
Inkling of the little boys
You pointed out to God –
Whose hymnbook-paper face

You drew a smile onto with hulking, off the
Pavement Labradors and giggles and with
Flushed and 'tut-tut' admonitions
That we only ever recognised as
Aunty's kindnesses?

At what kind point
Did God scratch out
The numbers you had found
(The chapter and the verse)
Whereby He might be
Daily contacted? Before
Or after you
Forgot yourself? Or

Do I, too, forget myself? Is
This too simple or too

Fine a cruelty
To comprehend
As if I had
The ear of God?

Melinda Lovell

Face to Face

My father, eighty four, shaves himself
slowly and calmly
without tremor
in front of a slightly mottled bathroom mirror
round and familiar
as a London Transport sign

It is a soothing ritual,
he rarely nicks himself
with his ancient kit –
no need to change it,
this razor is perfectly adequate,
this little wooden handled brush a treat

When I was seven maybe – if that –
I used to become absorbed, intently
watching him. Pyjama-clad,
using that dinky shaving brush
he'd cover chin and cheeks with lather
and then I'd wait patiently
for cheeks and chin to come back,
the razor rather like a snow plough
accumulating drifts
to be sloughed off in lukewarm water
a few economic inches
in a Shanks basin

I was joining in
with my father's reflection first thing
and if his eyes smiled
those crinkly lines I liked
collected at their far corners.
It was all right to be there
hearing birdsong and steam train
but no words said
and my small owl gaze
not in any way minded

Francis O'Gorman

The Touching Distances of Joyce's *Pomes Penyeach*

James Joyce's *Pomes Penyeach* (1927) ruminates on how distances can still touch. It allows the reader to think about on the capacity of the far-off, in multiple forms, to move; and it opens up the suggestive meanings of distances measured not only in physical or chronological terms but in mental space. And, so doing, Joyce's easily forgotten collection of thirteen brief poems offers a concentrated vision of the nature of exile not merely as a political or cultural concept, but as one refracted into a range of familiar and sorrowful human situations as well as, daringly, into the reading experience itself. Considering these elements of *Pomes Penyeach* is, in one way, simply to reveal the density of a local theme that holds this brief volume thematically and linguistically together. But, in another, it is to reveal how the play of distance in *Pomes Penyeach* enables the reader to face, albeit unobtrusively, some of the largest challenges and sensations in reading Joyce as a writer altogether: a writer for whom the reader's apparent distance from the text is a persistent enigma and sometimes a source of conflict in the interpretation of meaning and the apprehension of feeling.

The brief lyrics of *Pomes Penyeach* refer, the reader will quickly deduce, to many personal scenes and private narratives. They have an almost-secret relationship with autobiography and seem to speak, primarily, to a private audience in possession of a key:

Tutto è Sciolto

A birdless heaven, seadusk, one lone star
Piercing the west,
As thou, fond heart, love's time, so faint, so far,
Rememberest.

The clear young eyes' soft look, the candid brow,
The fragrant hair,
Falling as through the silence falleth now
Dusk of the air.

Why then, remembering those shy
Sweet lures, repine
When the dear love she yielded with a sigh
Was all but thine?

Trieste, 1914 [1]

To whom is this addressed? Is this story of almost-obtained love staged or 'real'? Is it imagined or autobiographical? The casual reader of poetry in 1927 could not answer. But there is an emotional and intellectual bridge still made between reader and this elegiac text despite the lack of private knowledge. The poem is neither entirely incomprehensible nor unaffecting. And the touching power of distance belongs more generally with *Pomes Penyeach*: it is part of the volume's theme as well as an apt description of the experience of reading it.

'Tutto è Sciolto', the words, are the entry point to the fifth poem: 'All is lost'. They invite an expectation of a negative, a desertion, a desert. And, indeed, the opening images flirt for a moment with emptiness – a birdless heaven, a lone star. But that is not all. The heart upon which the poem muses is not, it seems, entirely lost: 'faint' and 'far' are no synonyms of radical absence. Memory fashions a connection. The 'clear young eyes' remain in words. They are not quite lost from the poem's language even if they have been lost in the real world. And poised at the close of the poem's memory is a new configuration of distance and proximity. The poet writes against his own text, asking why he should 'repine', even in the act of repining, when he remembers that the 'dear love' had nearly been his. That love, he says of himself in the distancing third person, was 'all but thine'. How minute is *that* distance, the smallest gap of the 'all but', which is, in love – everything? Closeness, distance, and the living sense of a continuing sensation are all economically clinched in those three terse monosyllables.

What, in ordinary experience, in ordinary speech or even in poetry, might most commonly be said to touch from afar? Moonlight, perhaps, or starlight? Reflected from conventionally female forms (the stars, the moon), such light is the lover's conventional ambiance. Saturated with romance, such far-travelling pale and nocturnal illumination reaches across great distances, as Elizabeth Jennings in 'Delay' (1956) knew well, turning a star's light into a sorrowful emblem of inopportune desire. Joyce's 'Alone' is aptly bathed in moonlight, the illumination of distances, too:

The moon's greygolden meshes make
All night a veil,
The shorelamps in the sleeping lake
Laburnum tendrils trail.

The sly reeds whisper to the night
A name – her name –
And all my soul is a delight,
A swoon of shame.

Zurich, 1916

And to that that distinctive nocturnal environment, the poet adds another re-
flected light embodying presence that is almost intangible; another configu-
ration of the touch of light with lightness of touch. In the words 'shorelamps
in the sleeping lake', that reflected light is 'in' the water and not. Such bright-
ness is only ambiguously 'present' in the lake, merely shining back from a
reflective surface: it is 'on' but not 'in.' The fine discrimination of conditions
is, too, something like the relationship between the poet and his present-but-
not-present lover at the conclusion, a woman who is even less 'there' than
reflected lamplight can really be said to be part of a lake. Joyce's second
stanza alters a sense of simply being 'Alone' into a subtler, painful, almost-
aloneness, where 'The sly reeds whisper to the night / A name'. Such whis-
pering might suggest Pan's pursuit of Syrinx and her transformation into a
bed of reeds. But the plainer point is the poet's feeling for a woman prompted
by nothing surer than the imagined whisper of her name. There 'is no resur-
rection from the past', Joyce said in an early poem from around 1900, found
in his brother Stanislaus's commonplace book. But what could survive from
a personal history, he went on, was an 'image of my love unclouded'. [2] In
'Alone', it is not even an image, but a conscious mishearing of a faint sound
that survives. What is fixed in words is the emotion that can be derived from
the slightest 'presence' of a name, the most flimsy connection with the past
through an imagined word.

Absorbed with the frailest of things, Joyce's 1927 collection returns to
edges, to the almost-gone to search out the multiple significance of what
remains. The volume proposes emblems of that readerly feeling that the
texts themselves are remote but not entirely so; that there is knowledge we
do not have, yet where that lack does not entirely impede our connection,
our intimacy. The poems persist, unemphatically, in facing us with distances
that can be bridged, however slightly. 'Frail the white rose and frail are /
Her hands', Joyce says in 'A Flower Given to My Daughter', dwelling for

a moment on the preciously fragile, on what can still, nevertheless, literally touch. In 'Watching the Needleboats at San Sabba', he fantasizes more imagined sounds – 'prairie grasses sighing: / *No more, return no more!'* – which have only the palest hold, like frail hands, on the real, yet still are poignant, moving, meaningful. There is more moonlight, the faint trace of remote presences, in 'Simples'. But in 'Nightpiece', there is a scintillating succession of fainter forms. It is as if Joyce, entranced by the power of things on the verge of absence, is cataloguing embodiments, accruing the vocabulary, of the almost-there; the almost-not-there:

Gaunt in gloom,
The pale stars their torches,
Enshrouded, wave,
Ghostfires from heaven's far verges faint illume,
Arches on soaring arches,
Night's sindark nave.

The light is only just present; visibility only just possible. A 'Ghostfire' must be that from which the flame of life has almost wholly vanished. And what phantom spark remains is far off anyway, illuminating, as much as it can, the 'far verges' of the heavens. Light could hardly be less present while still being there. The natural and architectural spaces conjured are huge – 'Arches on soaring arches,' 'Night's sindark nave' – and so the spectral form of a dead light can 'fill' space with illumination that is almost inconceivable as light at all. It would be hard to imagine greater faintness, lesser presence, which is, nonetheless, still presence. And who or what can see their way in such obscurity? Aptly, metre changes from line to line, as if resisting a familiar pattern so that the reader cannot acoustically guess what is coming next, or find their way aurally with a pattern. And readers may well lose their way in the syntax too, struggling to work out if 'wave' is the main verb; struggling to decide what, precisely, is the principal noun; how, precisely, the sense flows. Yet flow it still does.

'Nightpiece' establishes a peculiarly concentrated repertoire of faintness that is still apparent to a perceiver, of the distant that is still discernible from afar. Joyce's exploration of states of near-impenetrability where all is not lost – 'Blind me with your dark nearness', he says in 'A Prayer' – become startlingly literal elsewhere. If *Pomes Penyeach* faces the reader, in a compacted form, with that peculiarly Joycean dilemma of not knowing exactly what 'background' information is needed to see a text clearly, the reader may realise with a wry smile that the 'background' to the eight-line 'Bahnhofstrasse' is blindness itself. At one simple level at least, we really do have to know something outside the poem to see it clearly:

> The eyes that mock me sign the way
> Whereto I pass at eve of day,
>
> Grey way whose violet signals are
> The trysting and the twining star.
>
> Ah star of evil! star of pain!
> Highhearted youth comes not again
>
> Nor old heart's wisdom yet to know
> The signs that mock me as I go.

Zurich, 1918

Eight lines, eight syllables in each line: the poem draws attention to the regularity of its lines, as befits a text about a Bahnhof, a railway station. But if the poem is visibly tidy, it concerns the nearly invisible as Joyce records his first attack of blindness. Facing that collocation 'eve of day,' it is tempting to see 'eye of day' just shorn of its all-important descender, as if the poem is affirming even in typography (you have to have good eyesight to see this) how small a loss can make an 'eye' something else. So the confusion of colour, the bleeding of terms into one another in the second stanza, mimics the poet's own bewilderment as he imagines an attempt to follow another one of the volume's stars, another emission of far distant light. Following a star has an unimpeachable biblical precedent. But the star that led the Magi is neither a star of evil nor of pain. The original image, reconceived in Joyce's poem, has become murky, almost impossibly hard to se – yet still after a fashion perceivable. If the biblical star portended revelation (and aptly 'Bahnhofstrasse' is conspicuously about signs), the faint glitter of light in a damaged eye portends not a miraculous birth, but the beginning of bodily age; a second childhood not a first. The signs are bad.

The poet sketches out in a mere fifty-four words a curious kind of exile from his own physical surroundings on Station Street. Peering through damaged eyes will not bring greater clarity, and yet something *is* still seen, despite optical disease, just as pity is still felt even by the reader does not know exactly the story 'behind' the poem. In such lines as 'Highhearted youth comes not again', Joyce reaches with the language of shared human sentiment accessible quite beyond the immediate history of his bodily decrepitude, to contact more ample, almost Yeatsian, almost proverbial verities. And other slim but moving contact is made across troubling distances in the bleak but brilliantly moving climax of what meanings 'exile' might bear in the volume: the poem, 'She Weeps Over Rahoon', a text that plays with a human sound that is there, and not there. 'There is an economic and there is a spiritual exile,' Richard Rowan reads in an article in *Exiles* (1918). Written by his friend and love rival Robert Hand, the article discriminates two different motives for leaving Ireland, insisting on both as forms of necessary choice: 'There are those,' Rowan reads, 'who left her to seek the bread by which men live and there are others, nay, her most favoured children, who left her to seek in other lands that food of the spirit by which a nation of human beings is sustained in life'.[3] That second conception is easily Joyce presenting his own decision in the best and most intellectual of lights. But *Pomes Penyeach* trades with subtler distinctions about what 'exile' might mean and who might feel it; with the emotional conditions that are not simply produced by leaving a country for economic or for spiritual reasons:

'She Weeps Over Rahoon'

Rain on Rahoon falls softly, softly falling,
Where my dark lover lies,
Sad is his voice that calls me, sadly calling,
At grey moonrise.

Love, hear thou
How soft, how sad his voice is ever calling,
Ever unanswered, and the dark rain falling,
Then as now.

Dark too our hearts, O love, shall lie and cold
As his sad heart has lain
Under the moongrey nettles, the black mould
And muttering rain.

Trieste, 1913

Written from a place of self-imposed distance from Ireland, 'She Weeps Over Rahoon' attends to another of the volume's distanced voices even as it echoes the end of *Dubliners'* 'The Dead' (1914). The voice calls faintly from the grave. Yet it is another ventriloquized sound, another imagined set of words that exist in the mind, projected onto the real, like the sound of rustling reeds mentally converted into a name. The voice in Rahoon (a cemetery in Galway) is present and absent; it is ever unanswered because the lover is dead; it is ever unanswered because there is no-one living to hear an answer. This voice is but a memory suffusing the landscape as the rain saturates it: it is real and unreal, present but impossibly and irretrievably absent. What lives in the mind has 'life' in an intimate but only metaphorical sense, however real the hope of hearing the dead again is. And the strange distances of love become part of the reading experience in a different way, too, as perceptual spaces are confused in the gap between the first two stanzas:

> [...] Sad is his voice that calls me, sadly calling,
> At grey moonrise.
>
> Love, hear thou
> How soft, how sad his voice is ever calling,
> Ever unanswered [...]

On first reading, that 'Love', beginning the third line, might seem as if it is an endearment addressed to the calling voice: is *this* the answer, perhaps, or at least a sign of communication, of exchange, in which the tomb is no barrier to the continuing conversations of love? But there is a shock, a realisation in the following line, with the personal pronoun, '*his* voice', that the lover (the person called 'Love') and the dead man are separate. There are two loves, and a woman caught between the past and the present, between two men, between the living and the dead, between what is here and what not. So to the question 'who is the woman's lover?' there is no straightforward answer. He who is far removed is confused in, inextricable from the present even though he is dead, and the poem's emotions involve plotting a course between the near and the far, the present and the almost-gone. How apt it is that Joyce's first line, 'Rain on Rahoon falls softly, softly falling' should be a chiasmus, as the poet tests in the subtlest level of word organisation how close two things can be while not being the same. '[Falls] softly, softly falling': the same words, the same meaning, yet different. Syntax taps out, teasingly, both proximity and difference, which is a microcosm of the emotional drama of the text.

'She Weeps Over Rahoon' brings to a climax the quirky absorption of *Pomes Penyeach* with the reader's experience of distance, and with what feelings and meanings may traverse it. Here is a collection intrigued by how a conception of 'exile,' tired though the word might be among Joyce's readers, can have astonishingly subtle emotional and mental meanings for a sensitive and suffering life. Marking out the most literal path of Joyce's exile in the dates and locations at the end of each poem, the volume nevertheless invites the reader to consider the most refined conception of distances, the idea of what crosses them, and how the business of living with distances in their many forms might be part of a familiar and even ordinary human predicament. In its searching of the sensations of distance, *Pomes Penyeach* opens up the power of the almost, of the nearly-gone, and of the vast distances that may lurk between things that seem close, and the closeness of things that seem vastly apart. Far from concerning merely what Robert Hand would call spiritual or economic exile, *Pomes Penyeach* deftly probes a sense of separation in many things, and examines the filaments that hold the separated together, as part of its lyrical essence: in love, in age, in illness, in mourning, in memory.

How easily readers may feel at a distance from Joyce's texts because they do not know a private history, a political event, a textual reference, the topography of a city. That is a persistent, creative, and demanding issue in reading Joyce. But *Pomes Penyeach* gives these issues a curious kind of answer because, within its disarming simplicity, the collection is entranced by the feelings and meanings that exist despite remoteness. *Pomes Penyeach* modestly suggests how readers can be strange 'exiles' from James Joyce's writing yet still know how faint presences can communicate and move. The tiny collection is not unique in Joyce's writing in revealing this. But it *is* special, I think, in the degree to which it transforms, with exceptional concision, that familiar Joycean experience into its own distinctive and self-conscious literary concerns.

[1] All references to *Pomes Penyeach* are to Joyce's *Poems and Shorter Writings* (London: Faber, 1991), pp.51-63. I use titles or poem numbers only.

[2] Ibid., p.79.

[3] James Joyce, *Poems and Exiles* (Harmondsworth: Penguin, 1992), p.245.

Sally Festing

Edwin Brock, an Enigma, (1927-1997)

'I believe that most activity is an attempt to define oneself… for me poetry, and only poetry, has provided that self-defining act' (*Here. Now. Always.*1977). Edwin Brock's creed could scarcely have been more cogent. The policeman, ad-man, father, lover, and half-suffocated child became a poet who wrote 14 books, one of them a volume of the Penguin series shared with Stevie Smith and Geoffrey Hill (Penguin Modern Poets 8, 1966). Through poetry, he was able to draw together the threads of a life that would otherwise have been alarmingly fragmented.

> There are many cumbersome ways to kill a man:
> you can make him carry a plank of wood
> to the top of a hill and nail him to it. To do this
> properly you require a crowd of people
> wearing sandals, a cock that crows, a cloak
> to dissect, a sponge, some vinegar and one
> man to hammer the nails home.
>
> ('Five Ways to Kill a Man')

Vibrant lyricism, strong rhythms, clarity and a sense of order, wry self-depreciatory humour and directness bordering on confessional were to be the hallmarks of work fêted by the Black Hill poets in the US and much anthologised. Brock's wife, Elizabeth, said that he knew what appealed to ordinary people. This doesn't detract from his standing; the craft was deadly serious to him.

For a poet of Brock's generation, his background was unusual. His potential for imaginative escape seems to have been developed early. Growing up the only child of working class parents in Peckham Rye could have been hopelessly crushed. He *was* crushed, both physically and by bullying, from time to time. Yet there grew in him an almost wilful determination to go his own way.

> Already I have learned not to want
> the things I want unless wanting
> should place it out of reach, so now
> I settle for something less than love:
>
> (*Here. Now. Always.* 1977)

At Alleyns School, gang warfare and lustful sexual experiment provided casual escape from loneliness. On leaving, Edwin spent an unrewarding year in the office of a timber-yard before being claimed by the Royal Navy. Two-years on a Destroyer didn't suit him either. He was fed up with the 'nauseating oily smell of ships' (*Here. Now. Always.*), but what he came to think of as the decisive episode in his life took place at the end of this term. Waiting in the Barracks at Hong Kong to be de-mobbed, he had read almost every dog-eared paperback in the library before turning to the *Penguin Book of Modern Verse*.

The find could hardly have been more momentous. T S Eliot's 'Rhapsody on a Windy Night' seemed to leap towards him from the page. 'I've seen the cat in the gutter… I know how he feels about dry geraniums, and the smell of chestnuts being roasted…' (*Here. Now. Always.*). He had often felt a failure; instead of hiding the fact, he would embrace and celebrate it in his own words.

Professing himself sick of discipline and uniforms, Brock must nevertheless have been attracted by something about working for the police. At 22 he had married Nellie Weller, so he needed a job. The move could also have been influenced by his challenging his step-father's wife-batterings. A constable, at any rate, is what he became. To some extent he was 'living a lie', but with a daughter born the first year of marriage and a son two years later, he was tied by obligation. Life held together, however tenuously, because he was writing and it offered him a measure of control. The most memorable day during his eight years in the constabulary could well have been the one on which he composed his first 'real' poem – 'Tragic Loss of Father in Boyhood' retitled 'When my father died'.

> On the day my father died
> > all the hoops in the neighbourhood rang
> > skate wheels shrilled on summer pavements
> > and I in my blakey-boots clanged one foot in each gutter

If the beauty and violence of those metal-toe and -heel protectors with their echoing long and short vowels suggest his flight to freedom, it wasn't that, so much as lack of personal involvement that left him unmoved by his father's sudden death (*Here. Now. Always.*). Poems continued to arrive. By the time a first collection was launched by the small but influential Scorpion Press (*An Attempt At Exorcism,* 1959) he had been a policeman for seven years and a poet for ten, with a track record in literary periodicals and weekly reviews. The father poem took first place.

James's Brock's death had spelt the end of a man who had flattened his son's ebullience with caution to behave decorously. Edwin was eleven at the time, and high on the rhythms of playground in pre-war London. But the situation was complicated by his being told his father had gone to hospital with a minor indisposition, so the news came as a shock. Angry at being deceived, he refused to bid farewell to a corpse that continued to haunt him, probably to *his* end. The poem was a rebellion. Its final couplet reconsiders the child's stance, affecting a softened attitude. These lines were added later for effect, the poet admitted; they were less truthful than the rest of the poem. But if 'When my father died' sees its protagonist as a nonentity to whom his son was more or less indifferent, nothing could have been further from the truth. Elsewhere, James is the 'smart Alec' who 'whistled at the wind' and 'threw bullseye darts in grinning public bars' ('Unlucky Jim'), and the man who insisted he should aim for grammar school ('In Memory of My Father'). Yet what is truth, what is artifice? Did truth mean fidelity to fact, truth as he wished it to be, or the friction between the two? Doesn't memory endlessly distort? Playfulness about the falseness of memory crops up in much of his work.

Other relations receive similar scrutiny. 'Poor old mother Brock', tattooed and possibly of Gypsy heritage, was cheap and 'loudly critical'. Gladys Brock (née Duffield) appears variously, unfulfilled, physically repressive, and negligent – a mother he never really 'got on with'.

An Attempt At Exorcism was published with the blessing of *The Times Literary Supplement*, the *New Statesman* and several other prestigious magazines as well as *The Observer* and *The Spectator*, journals in which favourable reviews followed. An authorial comment on the back strengthened Brock's stand as a non-academic contributor to serious poetry. 'I believe, with Hemingway, that the writer's task is to describe honestly and economically that small facet of reality which it is his privilege to enjoy … seeing the world in a grain of sand, rather than heaven in a wild flower'. Nothing was arch or consciously poetic. He seldom used two syllables where a good Anglo-Saxon word of one syllable would do. As Anthony Thwaite writes in a letter poem, his friend had 'A voice I'd never try to emulate – / Now there's a word you'd never ever use,' ('For Edwin Brock'). The title poem evokes a sunny image of an early girlfriend :

Now it is your yellow dress and young
sun-coloured legs that I remember
and the Old Bridge in Dulwich Park
and the ducks being noisy about summer.

But maybe the romantic vision never existed. Perhaps only the ducks were factual.

A policeman-poet was newsworthy. Local coverage of PC258's poeticising captured a BBC television interview and readings on the BBC Third Programme. The real perk was from Alan Pryce-Jones, editor of the TLS: the poems had 'outstanding quality'.

During the years on his native beat, Brock was forging lifelong friendships with poets like Peter Porter. Making headway in literary circles, he attended at least one meeting of The Group before deciding that his poetic part too, must be forged alone. By the end of the decade, anyway, he knew that anything else he did would be subservient to poetry. Indeed, publication may have been the impetus behind his decision to make changes in his lifestyle. The policeman's lot had not been altogether a happy one; as an advertising copywriter with Mather and Crowther at least he would be playing with words. Capitalising on praise received for *Exorcism*, Scorpion Press brought out a pamphlet of sonnet sequences in which he continued to explore his reactions to those closest to him.

> Only in love are lovers found
> and pains and pleasures in their limbs
> are love; only in love are sins
> allowed that end where love is bound.
>
> (*A Family Affair,* 1960)

If the new poems don't have quite the same sensory wildness, they find him one of those rare poets capable of abstract reasoning in and through verse.

The early sixties saw the beginning of a 35-year association with *Ambit,* a magazine that began as it meant to continue, publishing the work of writers and artists with whom the public was not familiar (Winter issue, 1960). On seeing No 2, Brock decided he could better the poems, and sent some in. Founding editor Martin Bax was swift to recognise a new voice. 'Certain Flowers', with its assured mixture of reason and song, made its debut in No 3.

> Certain flowers fold in
> upon themselves at night,
> and we interpret this
> as something physical;
> this way all problems reconcile
> themselves, like flowers, to darkness.

'A marvellous poem' says Bax, who fast became a friend. By Issue No 13, Brock was poetry editor.

In the meantime, the Brock's twelve year marriage had foundered. After he discovered his wife with her paramour, she disappeared leaving the children, and he was left to cope. He had met at work, the artist Elizabeth Skilton, and by coincidence she was moving to Sydenham from where she was able to offer a measure of support. Personal confusions continued to inform much of Edwin's work: an unhappiness confirmed in a third collection (*With Love from Judas,* 1963). Divorce didn't take place for another year after endless haggling over the children's custody. Andrea (1949) and Nicholas (1951) were ten and twelve at the time, a responsibility that permeated self-questioning poems such as 'An arrangement for seeing Children' and 'Catastrophe'.

> There are times
> when I feel a kind of Eichmann of cats,
> and pray that it will not be the same
> with wives.
>
> ('Catastrophe')

Social conscience propelled by humanism was to inspire some of Edwin Brock's best known work. 'Five Ways to Kill a Man' was written quickly after hearing Britten's War Requiem. It ends disarmingly, 'There are, as I began, cumbersome ways / to kill a man. Simpler, direct, and much more neat / is to see that he is living somewhere in the middle / of the twentieth century, and leave him there.' The flat tone is chilling. Thwaite describes 'An unforgettable blend of the laconic and the serious in what became instantly recognisable as the Brock voice' (*Five Ways To Kill A Man,* 1990, back cover).

Another way to prick the conscience was to reduce world problems to animal proportions. A poem could then present an acceptable image of a frightening reality. 'The Song of the Battery Hen' was written in the wake of Rachel Carson's *Silent Spring* and the tide of rising unease about the environment and concerns the exploitation of animals. Brock was amused to hear lines in the voice of his pitiful Pertelote quoted on *The Archers*: 'We can't grumble about accommodation ... I am in the twelfth pen / on the left-hand side of the third row / from the floor'. Besides animals, he used references from TV, Gandhi, Marriage Guidance and the first run of self-help manuals, anything that hinged on contemporary concerns. Plain prose enabled him to think clearly, and his advertising experience was taking effect in short chopped lines, their emphasis reinforced by pungent internal rhyming. There was a barbed usefulness in marketing language:

inasmuch as you
will climb to heaven
 on a neighbour's neck
I will sell you spiked climbing boots.
>   (*Contemporary Poets of the English Language*, 6th ed., 1996)

or

Ban the bomb ban
the bomb ban the
bomb ban the bomb
>   ('Symbols of the Sixties').

Edwin Brock was a devotee of West Coast jazz, and his name had appeared in North American magazines since the early 60s, but it was through Dr Bax that his work came to the attention of James Laughlin, wealthy and influential editor of *New Directions* who discovered such substantial poets as William Carlos Williams. Laughlin published five of his collections in the avant garde and prestigious Prime Premier series, among which, a 'collected' in 1972 was followed by a publication from Capra Press in California (*I Never Saw It Lit*). The *Penguin Modern Poet* (1966) had given him more promotion than any other publication, inclusion had been a decisive accolade. Laughlin's publications made him one of few British poets of his time to be noticed by the Americans.

Critics traced his work to Dylan Thomas, Graves, Larkin, Blunden, Hughes, Hardy and Blake. 'To find a common factor in that lot, you have to be … another critic!', the poet said. (Contemporary Poets of the English Language, 6th ed., 1996). Howard Sargeant reckoned he was influenced more by American than by British poets, both in the 'confessional style' and in the adoption of short lines. Some of his allegiances may have been American. Martin Bax remembers an enthusiastic sharing of Galway Kinnell's eccentrically-named twelfth collection (*The Avenue bearing the initial of Christ into the New World*). But Brock read widely and was largely his own man. In his first volume he had found a voice drawn from the syntax and diction he heard around him in South London and the lyrics of singer song-writer and folk musician, Woody Guthrie. The leaning towards confessional was a matter of inclination and background.

Sound was a vital ingredient in all his writings; the novel (*The Little White God*, Hutchinson, 1962), television and radio plays drawing on his police experience, a hilarious book of poems for children (*Fred's Primer*, Macmillan, 1969) dedicated to his daughter with Elizabeth, Sally or 'Fred', and aptly illustrated by Elizabeth, and the potpourri of prose and poems that form his autobiographical fragments of childhood. The last might be less compelling than his pure verse volumes but it too lends itself to being read aloud. One is left with the consciousness that poetry's concentration and form - its edges and silence, were necessary to his art.

Not surprisingly for a man whose oddities, instincts and ambiguities produce a bizarre portrait, he was drawn to and repelled by religion. It was his awareness of 'something wanted / I do not understand' (*Here. Now. Always.*) that prompted him to befriend a parish priest who confirmed him in March 1955 in St Paul's church, Forest Hill. Religious ambiguity was not altered by taking the sacraments, 'religion is not a necessity' ('Walking with Neighbours'), but God features in a lot of his 60s poems. In 'Portraits and the Poses', God is abandoned for 'bicycles, filmstars, Glen Miller/and my penis', yet he admitted

> superstitiously
> I touch prayer
> to make
> a photograph
> for God
> to love.
>   ('Five Exposures')

Edwin once admitted that being a policeman was a bloody awful job but he may not have thought the same about advertising (Les Williamson, Memorial speech), at the same time, he stood a little apart from it. Thwaite says, 'He was cleverer than almost any of them at identifying the market, piercing through layers of fancy bullshit, to sell'. (*The Independent Obituary*, 10.9.1997). He coined phrases such as 'Pub Grub' and 'Suck. Squeeze. Bang. Blow' – the firing sequence of a 4-cylinder car engine, and worked in collaboration with Alan Rodford on a famous campaign for the *Financial Times*. 'No FT. No comment'. The paper's circulation zoomed, and the phrase went into *Low Speak, a Dictionary of Criminal and Sexual Slang*.

PR agencies regularly change their names and/or get taken over by each other. Brock joined Ogilvy, Benson & Mather through a take-over, shortly before it reverted to being Ogilvy & Mather. The practice was to work in teams or 'creative groups', which was where he met David Ryland in the late 70s. 'It was a cut-throat industry', David remembered, 'He must have had a tough streak, and the firm appreciated his input since they allowed him to work part time. While living with his mother in Camberwell's Jephson Street, from time to time he stepped on the north-bound Norwich train and slipped on his writing hat.'

In 1969 Edwin and Elizabeth moved to Norfolk's Brundall; seven years later, to The Granary in a wing of an old white clapboard mill over the River Tas. From the meeting place of road, river and railway surrounded by water meadows, the Granary balcony looks straight down on the mill pool with its picturesque leaky punt. Perceiving that there are certain landscapes in which you feel the bones of the earth, Edwin became tuned to the play of sun and season.

> Now it is this humid July afternoon.
> Curtained by willows and willowherb
> and lulled by the background music
> of an idyllic mill race
>
> ('Fuckerduck')

'He possessed the Tas', said Anthony Thwaite who lives with Anne almost next door, in the handful of houses that make up the settlement (quoted in *Literary Norfolk*, Earwaker & Becker, 1998). 'I took to him immediately, convivial, sometimes reckless; but always gentle, generous, tough, funny, entertaining, lovable' (*The Independent* Obituary, 10.9.1997). Among poems dedicated to various people, the Thwaites received a quietly reflective one ('Walking with neighbours'). It was in the late 70s, with 'The River and The Train', we get a measure of inner peace that jogs the poetry into what Peter Porter described as the 'extraordinarily pure, almost abstract language' of his final collection (*Contemporary Poets of the English Language*, 6th ed., 1996).

In retirement (1988), Brock spent more time doing things he enjoyed – Bonsai gardening, painting and creating beautifully-shaped pots. He worked hard at his hobbies because he liked doing things well and all fed into the poems. In 1993 he had a stroke; for several weeks he lost his memory and almost his ability to speak. The effect of words recurring is potent in a poem honed back to the fear that spilled in.

> Someone had murdered someone
> somewhere again. It was a black space
> running away from fear
> and I did not know how much to give it.

It was not dying but death
of love. And not one love
but everything. It was like trying
to go straight through
from one fear to another
without love.
It was abandonment.

Death and fear simmer through the teasingly titled 'On the first stroke' from *And Another Thing*. 'Love' features three times, even if each conjures its withdrawal. Never had the love and companionship of his wife of 30 years seemed more at stake. He knew about 'abandonment'; it was something he'd felt as a child. 'You were always abandoning me' he once charged his mother (*Here. Now. Always.*). Mortality pricks the edges of the white space, though the poet is nothing if not – by the skin of his teeth – all here. Threading through the damage, the worry, and coastal altitude is the languor of Frankie Laine: 'Someone was singing Do not forsake me / O my darling. It is for later.' The refrain is picked up toward the end of this poem, and once more in an intense love song that closes the final collection ('Ringed by the flat horizon'). The only possible debt I detect is to the stuttering seriousness of WS Graham.

It is always becoming dark
and I am worried that the ladies
allow me to walk from one night to another
with no-one to look after me.
I am afraid and pull the black blanket up
to just below my eyes and look over it.
('On the first stroke')

The Brock who was very much alone is simultaneously part of his time and place, a sharer with whom anyone can identify. It's the directness again, the sense of a voice speaking straight to the reader that keeps the poems fresh. In the event, a remarkable recovery sparked four prolific years in which he delved into the experience and its aftermath. From Tharston he haunted the windy North coast with its cliff road from Cromer running between the sea and the hospital. In a hotel on Blakeney Marshes, the guns of wild fowlers woke him to new hopefulness. We can't but feel that his acceptance released new energies in his writing. Eeven after cancer of the pancreas was diagnosed, he continued to write says Thwaite, who edited the posthumous book.

Brock died in Low Tharston, almost seventy years old, and seldom had the world felt more beautiful. There were seven readers at his memorial gathering; five poets and two PR colleagues. A video of the occasion begins with the youthful poet reading 'Five Ways to Kill a Man'. I hadn't expected his voice to be as gentle, though it was a quality mentioned by others. (Alan Rodford spoke of the FT being 'charmed by his gentle and un-addy style'.) Gladys Brock's second marriage produced two more children, giving Edwin three siblings, all much younger. The reading was followed by Edwin's brother Michael's excerpt from the autobiography. 'Little boy / one day / you will walk among her words / without falling.' The 'her' referred to was his mother.

Note:

The author would like to thank Martin Bax, Anthony Thwaite, Elizabeth Brock and David Ryland for help with this piece.

Omar Sabbagh

Worldliness far from Cynicism, on Marilyn Hacker's *Names* and *Essays On Departure*

To want substance in cognition is to want a utopia.
It is this consciousness of possibility that sticks to the concrete, the undisfigured.

Theodor W. Adorno, 'Introduction,' Negative Dialectics

Exiles, at least, have clarity of purpose:
can say my town, my mother and my fate, my country.

from 'Ghazal: dar al-harb'

As the epigraphs above intimate, there is a very strong case for saying that true 'Otherness' isn't truly occluded as Other. The otherness or adequate transcendence Adorno invokes belongs in a sense only to God. This (very poetic) philosopher wishes for an Adamic naming, an (*impossible*) Adamic concept, where thing and word are immanently one. Similarly, the poet's 'clarity' is the clarity of those 'beyond' the Pale.

A woman, a feminist, a (*non-Zionist*) Jew, a lesbian, Marilyn Hacker partakes of this paradox. 'Epiphanous' or 'ephemeral' ('Lauds'), mise-en-abyme or thoroughgoing Adamic closure, age and innocence, hope and despair, agency and impotence, among many of the woven and processual dichotomies which inhabit this collection – there is a sense in which Hacker's poetic persona is an Other to (her own) Otherness. So when she writes in the final stanza of 'For Kateb Yacine':

Exiles filling the breach of winter days
with rhetoric have nothing, but have time
for rhetoric as logical as rhyme...

What's tautly intimated is the reparation or redemption which form enacts for loss, privation or otherness in whatever facet – form, like language itself, being an-other kind of Otherness to the meat of feeling.

One of the themes and techniques to be discussed is ambiguity; but it is read from the perspective of the boon of ambiguity or textuality: thus, semantic drift and slippage are made an executive choice, a strategic deployment of the author's 'consummate style' ('Ghazal: Style'). What I am suggesting is that any fallen babble is the product of a sovereign imagination. Indeed, as well as being filled with ghazals, sonnets, gloses, translations, there is a taut symmetry of symmetry and asymmetry which inhabits the architecture of the collection. There is both a tapering at the end of the collection, involving inverse repetition of stanzaic forms and thematic content (titled or not), as well as similar symmetries within the purlieus of each of the four sections. This doubled feature itself is a doubling of symmetry or harmonisation, suggesting a surfeit beyond them. But more than that, the penultimate piece (though last in her *New and Selected*) is emblematic; 'Ghazal: Begin' confirms and unhinges the paradox under consideration: it is an ending which is about beginning; there is a sense of closure and coming full-circle, and a sense of the dovetailing, the baton-passing, or 'family-likeness' nature of passing or serial time, however much garnered into form and verse.

The way I'd like to enter into a commentary of the work in this collection is cognate with Herbert Marcuse's notion, in an essay in his *Negations*, that poetry is much like 'dialectical' thought. In tandem with this, there is my own teasing hermeneutic of the phenomenology of inversion, which in fact is glaringly highlighted in one of the ghazals in this collection.

Dialectical thought, to cash it out simply, is not only thought, but immanently, the thought of thought. Which is to say, for Kant, understanding or cognition involved a subject and an object, intransitively related. Hegel's basic insight was to say: so, yes, I think this or that thing – but as soon as I say or think of this I am at the same time thinking of the thinking of that thing. Thus subject becomes object and object becomes subject. The difference might be put this way: for (Kantian) understanding one can 'think' of/about 'God'; for Hegel's sublime Reason one 'thinks God', transitively as it were. Thus, at the end of 'Lauds', Hacker writes:

Now, maculated by some matinal
buttered bread, or coffee, while it rained
outside, its gesture is a curve, embrace
of what's within the arc, time within place.

The gesture is the gesture of 'praise'. And, like Augustine in his *Confessions,* the mystical insight is that love or praise precedes and grounds cognition or understanding, or, far better: representation. Let me now detail just a sample of some of the dialectical (in the more prosaic sense) processes in this collection. In 'Pomegranate' then:

After years' displacements, the words risk having
a double meaning –

risk, or have the luck of a double meaning
in their roots. Some words have their own ideas,
so a line with bullets in it transforms them
deftly, to sparrows.

Or, say, in 'Paragraph' at the end of the first section:

The father who outlived his daughter writes
something about the snow...
... cold as a monument, the daughter
who outlived her father thinks...

We would normally associate the sense of risk or urgency with unction,
thus with laden meaningfulness and gravitas. And yet here the risk is the
risk in subverting a sovereign auctoritas. And we would normally associate
luck with the opposite of emplotment or the justification that leads to a sense
of necessity. But here luck is 'radical', a ligament to root reality. In this
verse, both aspects of the ambivalence inhabit each other paradoxically, as
paradoxically as the father/daughter minuet.

One way of thinking of dialectical thought is to say that, even if in its
absence, it is constituted by the view of the whole, as opposed to the serial
or atomistic. In a sense, to be dilated upon below in varied ways, an inverted
consciousness inhabits this 'Utopia' (Adorno, *Negative Dialectics*) or
embodies the 'Thing' (Lacan, *Seminar VII*) which is the precondition *and*
product of being *both* subject and object immanently. However empirically
absent, the whole or total(ising) con-text is that which allows for the gambit of
meaning (even if empirically dilative or textual) at all. However discursively
unreachable, the Other of the Other lacks nothing, is not spurred into the
danger or risk of a sublunary other, Is That It Is (to paraphrase), turns on
itself. This does not mean that all is resolved, but rather that it is what puts
into relief the lack of resolution of the (other) world. I will approach instances
of strategically deployed ambiguity, slippage and drift which are products
of this kind of composure, presently. But a few of the charged dichotomies
which are set into relief by this subject-object position, are here briefly
elicited. Or, otherwise put, the mise-en-abymes I now detail, are precisely
based on an Adamic 'naming', names which don't redeem because they are
the naming of the self-named. Let me explain this fallen-ness of the unfallen.

Opening the collection, 'Ghazal: In Summer' starts with city streets 'crowded with possibility'. We progress through peopled and colourful scenes, with the penultimate couplet dubbing the 'oligarch', the author of illicit violence. It closes with:

Let them not, in Maryam's name or Marilyn's,
blot any cindered city off a graph in summer.

The poet is naming names who themselves (poets) have been busy with naming and/or continue to name. Or, cognate, closing an-other opening poem (of the second section: 'An Ocean Between Us'):

The morning light spells its name on my white coffee cup
but it aches with absence: *there is an ocean between us*.

Here light (white) is spent and imposes its name upon 'white', but aches (privation) like that white which is absence, air or distance. 'Metaphor' is used as metaphor ('Ghazal: Across the Street'). White is a name for the whiteness of names. Indeed, the last couplet of 'Ghazal: The Beloved' ironises and instantiates romance (form).

You are promised release on the recognizance
(will this be a redemptive clause?) of the beloved.

The re-cognizance is of the essence: an end questioning its own end-status because it is an end. This playful but profound ghazal is dedicated to Faiz Ahmed Faiz, and the play with closure or integration is based on Faiz's response in an interview to the question: 'What is poetry?' He replied that it is that which remains after the loss of the beloved.

Or, alternatively, witness the illicit names in 'For Kateb Yacine' and 'Ghazal: *dar al harb*', which are the precondition of 'naming', regulating or directing one's reality; the condition of agency, or meaningful action and results.

… We all had pseudonyms,
code-names, pet-names, pen-names: *noms de guerre,*
simple transliterations, unfamiliar
dipthongs in rote order, palindromes
and puns patched on the untranslatable
(unuttered, anguished) root of a syllable.

Where will justice and peace get the forged passports
it seems they'll need to infiltrate my country?

It's as if that otherness which is transgression is the only (desperate) source of a potential identity which might give the law to it-self, or make its acts cohere. It's as if something essentially fictive is the prerequisite to gaining purchase on the practical world.

Ending the eponymous sonnet-sequence 'Names', the eighth sonnet invokes a victim dubbed as 'Nobody'. Every-thing is the same as No-thing. The condition of a plethora of worldly places is, thus, that seemingly God-like position which is 'No-Place'. The condition of dispersive ambiguity is that 'clarity' mentioned in one of the epigraphs to this article, which is executive and filled with and by self-contained intents. Good examples, then, of strategic ambiguity:

Above the frieze of chimneys, antennas and window gables,
swallows in V-formation used to soar across the street.
('Ghazal: Across the Street')

A scent of hyacinth clings to your fingers,
of sap from a broken leaf, of moss, of the beloved.

Ambiguous...
('Ghazal: The Beloved')

a dialogue with mistranslated text,
a tense the narrative poises, perplexed,
upon...
('For Kateb Yacine')

In the first an image of nature is perhaps used to figure a (very un-natural) form of mechanised violence. But more than this: note the potential polymorphous-ness of 'used'. It might mean simply the imperfect: the sense that swallows were wont to.... Or, alternately, it might have the slim suggestion of natural innocence, how the swallows 'were'. Finally – indeed this very slippage is a microcosm of my whole present critique – it may have the sense of the image being 'used' by the poet to figure her (ambiguous or not) imaginary. The syntax in the second jars against the romantic resolution of loved and 'beloved'. The scent is of 'moss' 'a broken leaf' and/or the 'beloved'. This slippery syntax in the list is then named as it were in the opening of the next stanza with 'Ambiguous...'. As if the author were following a line of thought in arrears to her-self. Finally, that 'poises' is masterly. It suggests with 'poise', or enacts poise by suggesting with 'poise', 'poses' and 'pauses'. Again, if you like a microcosm or synecdoche of the structure of feeling I've tried to tease out so far.

144

As an-other kind of concentrate of all the above, witness the self-reflective form and content in 'Ghazal: Myself'. Opening and ending then:

> They say the rules are: be forgotten, or proclaim myself.
> I'm reasonably tired of that game, myself…

> A signature hangs unwritten, below the last
> line on the page, where I'm obliged to name myself.

The author is playing/forming many (formal) games with form here. The ghazal is of course a form distinguished by the poet signing his or herself at the end, naming his or herself, which reflexivity might be thought, quite glaringly, as congruent with the whole notion of form itself, or euphony. The 'myself' is the Self which deploys the antinomies of self-relation, self-revelation and that which is 'unwritten', like the line-break between 'last / line'. And so on… The Self is the self that names itself and the self that names the (self-making) other to its Self.

Throughout the collection, scenes of far-flung places and legions of persons, of the Other, are loaded with an aura of wide journeying and felt experience and worldliness in the best sense. There are moments where variety of place or of persons, differences in 'space' are vehicles for the spurring dissonances in time, or, rather, fulfilled time, storied time. This means time which is not just an 'ephemeral' open-ended process of mortality, but rather the time made the poet's 'own', time undergone now become time possessed. 'A moment jumps the interval; the next / second, a sudden dissonance swells up', opens 'For Kateb Yacine'. Opening the action it is redolent with that intransitivity, that 'election' or choice which denotes true agency, even if the agency, like Lawrence Durrell's 'tree of idleness', is one busy with 'waiting' as one of Hacker's Ghazals has it. Indeed, Hacker seems to me in the very tradition of the Francophone Durrell, (or his cohorts, Miller and Nin); think of the palimpsests and relativity of *The Alexandria Quartet*: 'time within place'; place or locus, 'which can mean, in context, / pilgrim, or exile' ('Pomegranate'). '[I]n context' – that hale and slippery thing'.

In the second poem of her *Essays on Departure: New and Selected Poems* (Carcanet, 2006), 'Feeling and Form', the creative act is viewed 'like an idea of movement, draw- / ing its shape from sequence'. Like Yeats's late-romantic 'dancer' spent in the dance, the whole is always in the process of being created, as lived out by that last processual line-break; it is also the very condition of that process. Without glossing one of the many 'Glosses' in this (latest) collection *(Names)*, it is enough to say that one of them opens with a formula which is a type of musical and metaphysical justice:

'A sibilant wind presaged a latish spring...'

*

As I began in bulk with Hacker's latest collection, *Names*, let me begin again here with the title of one of the earliest selections in *Essays on Departure*. Her excerpted 1985 collection is titled *Assumptions*. And reading the selected poems from this collection, I discerned many meanings for this: first, one has the traditional religious sense from Christian revelation, Mary rising, pure as pure can be to heaven. This has both serious intent and ironic intent, as we shall see. Then there's the idea of 'redeeming' lived experience via its formation or organisation in verse. Then there are, perhaps, the 'assumptions' so native to the young, put into relief by re-cognizing verse. The most interesting sense I've scented though, is perhaps Hacker's brilliant (poetic) critique of the assumptions straight people, or those dominating a society's discourse and self-image, have about being gay. What's so brilliant about Hacker, and so refreshing, is that she is not aesthetically 'alternative', in fact her aesthetic is very much centered and centric. If she is Romantic, it is by being universal, speaking as Wordsworth had it the 'language of (wo)men'; and it certainly is not a whining preciousness attendant upon difference, like some 'beautiful soul', exceptional only because (s)he is exceptionalist!

In a way this last reading ties-in all the previous ones. Like religious discourse, she assumes and expresses a meta-narrative, a fundamental union and communion of all types. By correcting her own or others' 'assumptions', she enacts a very public cause and boon. And finally, though of course highlighting herself as a 'Jewish lesbian in France', (the recitative of 'Graffiti from the Gare Saint-Manqué') her voice and sensibility is able to carry this, either with seriousness or with irony, because she seemingly considers (and laughs at) herself as just as different or the same as anyone. True of course, and refreshing.

The main way this is expressed in this early collection is by her conversational tone, which is eminently inviting, and yet far from prosaic. This conversation is either the source of her work, or, via dialogic insertions, part of the content. Which is to say, she is not dictating or shrieking at her reader; she's simply too at ease with her-self. After all (from *Open Windows*), 'A matrifocal world would comprehend / compassion, dignity, and common sense'... Either by skilfully mocking a queer theorist and 'she-Academician', or by having vivaciously lightsome lines like: '...We have Reagan. Why not be / another Jewish Lesbian in France?' (from *Grafitti*...) – Hacker takes herself, and us, seriously enough not to be too serious. Like her storied grandmother in 'The Little Robber Girl Gets On in the Wide World', Hacker, then as now, and for all her consummate technical skill, seems 'fonder / of talk than of fire'. In fact, as well as having an epigraph for an earlier piece from H.C. Andersen, this latter piece intentionally invokes that ancient kind of 'assumption' which is the fairytale form. And this is directly contiguous with what I've said so far. The beauty of the fairytale – and its success depends on it – is, as G.K. Chesterton was wont to argue, that the marvelous episodes, the wonder and the romance, the 'otherness', is only effective if the hero or heroine is 'ordinary' – a man or woman among men and women. If one inhabits one's self without housed-ness or ease, if one is obtrusively other, then the fairy-tale of everyday life comes across as boring or dull, too much like one's morbid self. One needs to be centered to see the value of difference, whether this latter inheres in the world, and is its mirror, or is its desideratum, its lamp; whether it fights mad assumptions extant in the world, or whether it helps us to ascend to a better, more peaceful, or 'common-sensical' world.

The 1986 collection, *Love, Death and the Changing of the Seasons* was originally a unified novel in verse, written with Meredith's *Modern Love* in mind as well as Shakespeare. It is only sampled in *Essays on Departure*. And yet, the poems in this selection, villanelles, (mainly) sonnets or sonnet-sequences, wistful missives, most addressing or apostrophizing a 'You', might also be read as finding their master-trope with the Metaphysicals. In particular, as I read them, there seem to be quite a few which parody the (p) lay of vulnerability and invulnerability evinced in Marvell's infamous 'To His Coy Mistress'.

At times, one senses the casualness (or *sprezzatura*) evident in the final lines in some of these early sonnets, as a kind of shield against and reflector of (the narrative of) involvement and desire. Indeed, though there is much sex, drugs, and rock and roll splayed and formed in the book, and though Hacker seems to be talking down the meta-physical – at the same time she is ever invoking it. Much like Augustine (sometime libertine, sometime saint), Hacker seamlessly inter-mixes two types of desire, *caritas* and *cupiditas*, which have one common root. As a gay woman and a consummate poet she is the God, and at the same time the worshipper. Thus in 'Runaways Café 1' when she writes, 'O bless and curse / what's waking up no wiser than it was', the blessing and the curse enact the paradoxical discourse of the whole sonnet, where transgression is avenue to the law, and law or form is the precondition of transgression.

There is a significant manner in which the voice behind and lived-out in these poems is both within the purview of the pleasure principle, and beyond it. In technical terms, vehicle and tenor both inhabit each other immanently and follow from each other. For instance, 'our house' and the pursuant 'mansion' (from the fifth sonnet of 'Eight Days in April') is both a concrete

147

image of lovers' harmony and an abstraction speaking to the female sex. And perhaps, within this scansion, 'man-sion' says something about the guilt or, later, 'grief' which is native to the expressing artist, one who gives more than (s)he takes: 'Grief, and I want to take it up in you', opens the sonnet so-titled. There's a fuzzy utopia for giving and taking.

In fact the poetic persona often imagines her lying lovers within their dreams, and achingly wonders. This suggests both the needy urgency of desire, and in a way, is of a piece with the god-like position of the artist – an Other of the Other. The fact that one is imagining – imagining – and in an imaginative form, is redolent with the feminine, and in particular, that very 'container' is 'contained' – all others becoming a form of self-relation, as though to be lesbian were to be doubly so! Thus: the continual dialectic. Indeed, images of water, of seas, of waves – mytho-poetically, the feminine – contrast with the ending of one of the later sonnets ('Five-thirty, little one, already light'), which holds more gravitas and wound-ability than the earlier playful bathos.

> And aren't we, when we are on dry land
> (with shaky sea legs) walking hand in hand
> (often enough) reading the lines on graves.

One hears embracing echoes, of course, of Marvell, but also of Donne, where death, via love, dies; where the changing seasons are so changing, and desire is as acutely sensual and pagan as it is, that both become a new form of stasis and decorum.

In *Going Back to the River* (1990) Hacker remains a consummate storyteller. While perhaps not biographically influenced by the-already-mentioned Francophone Durrell, Miller, Nin, my suggestion of similarity is lived out in this instance. Whether it's the commemoration of the commemorating eighty-four year-old Elizabeth in 'Dinner With Elizabeth', or the idiosyncratic characters introduced in medias res in the Pound-imitation 'Nights of 1962: The River Merchant's Wife' – scenic quidditas is the thing. The characters which populate the verse are introduced impressionistically: which is to say, following Ford Madox Ford (who was following the likes of Maupassant), when a character enters the narrative he or she enters on an exaggerated or Titanic note: the large impression is made on the reader; a worldliness. And this sense of singularity as filled with universal appeal, or alternatively of loss as the prerequisite of configuring memory, is embodied in lines, say, from only one of the 'river' poems in this selection:

Out of the smallest, oldest perched village
branch well-marked paths, beside the stream, the ravine.

The streams flow down into the local river.
The footpaths widen into roads back here.

I lived upriver from a different harbor.
Let's say the boat left without me....

The highway spared the hill town it bypassed.
I can still get there, leave there overland.

                    ('Going Away from the River')

Land, as opposed to the eponymous river, signifies the texture of earning one's values; being lost, at a loss, obtrusively hindered by solid matter, is part of the way one attains the salutary meanings of one's experience, so unlike the snaky ease of travelling upon a sleek river. If the boat had not left without her, if it had been smooth sailing, the poem would not have come into existence. The river is something one partakes of only if one is 'going back' to it, *post festum*.

Throughout this selection, rivers stand of course for mortality and the seamlessness of time, the seamlessness between poet and poem, and of then and now. Indeed in 'Les Serpillières' we shift from poet to her mother via an objective correlate, a bit like the serpentine Proustian 'madeleine'. The rivers are also (to continue with the narrative note), one's life's course, one's destiny:

When you were young, it guarded and promised you
  that you would follow other rivers
oceans away from a landlocked childhood.

                    ('Going Back to the River')

And yet destiny can be both something that *happens to* one and something one ploughs for oneself. In 'Nights of 1962: The River Merchant's Wife' and in 'Separate Lives', there is river-ing, there is journeying across peopled time, and yet both involve repetition and coming full-circle between their openings and endings. This lives-out the very conceit of 'going back' to the river, re-membering memory. Which is to say, a paradoxical utopia:

And if I'd died and lived to tell the tale,
recovered from the knowledge I'd recover,
I looked a little less like death warmed over.

                    ('Separate Lives')

Thus the meta-physics continues. As ever, for Hacker love and desire are discovered as both salves to passing mortality, and as its very index. One must die to live to tell the tale. The boat on the river must abandon one to rugged, jagged land, in order for one to earn the return to the river. The boat on the river must abandon one to the tough roughage of clunky, bruising land, in order for one to earn the origin of, and the originating of, the coursing (of) verse.

The selection from *Winter Numbers* opens on a poem – detailing the sadness at lovers' and friends' deaths of cancer and AIDS – is titled, 'Against Elegies'. Let me begin with four associations, apart from the sense of number as poetic meter or the metrical.

First, this collection having its end (purpose) as death, the title intimates the pat phrase 'your number's up', and/or the listing/numbering of the dead: legions of legionnaires. There is also the sense of the list of the loved and passed as having been (and/or re-confirmed by death as) 'numéros'. Against 'elegy', a stance against the sense of ending or purpose being allotted to miserable death, Hacker is at-one with the 'Against Interpretation' of Susan Sontag. Finally this poem opens *Winter Numbers*, just as that notorious wintry discontent opens Shakespeare's *Richard III*. Other poems which invoke ending, however meaningful or meaningless, are 'Nearly a Valediction', 'Chiliastic Sapphics', 'Year's End', 'Cancer Winter' and the dusk of 'Dusk: July'.

For Aquinas, the angels were – each one of them – a species to his/herself. Thus Heaven or Utopia is the ultimate conundrum and paradox: a society of absolute individuals. When Hacker writes in 'Against Elegies', 'For every partisan', 'I can only bear witness for my own / dead and dying, whom I've often failed', she is being wintrily realistic and humble. One cannot love 'humanity' unless one is a prophet or a saint. One loves humanity in a partisan way, through one's lovers, friends, family. One's bearing witness to death by song is both 'irrelevant' and 'amazing' ('Year's End') – exemplary and so non-sensical as to be uncomprehendingly unique. Indeed, 'Chiliastic Sapphics', starts in conclusive vein on 'Sunday afternoon at the end of Summer', and 'ends', with the poet naming her particular moment in medias res, and with the contingent detail of her surroundings: the end is less an end than the commencement.

Sense is inverted throughout this selection, much like the paradoxes in 'Against Elegies', which are not only expressed by that very title, but also by the detailing within the poem of how the older sixty-something generation continue to survive and live resplendently, while the younger thirty/forty-something's die unnaturally from cancers and viruses. The age-old form of keening elegy is both apposite and not so, given that youth dies before age.

There are of course other selections within this book. However, the directing motifs of my discussion are just as pertinent for – if very far from exhausting – the work not considered here. One omission from my selective commentary, of course, is any consideration or overview of the prolific translations Hacker has made of the likes of Venus Khoury-Ghata or Claire Malroux among others, since the mid-1990s.

Simply put, Hacker's worldliness and the vital rainbow of her palette are far from cynicism. They come across throughout with an aura of wonder and awe: a radical innocence, rather than a snake a-chomp upon its own tail – which might well have been a telltale. In this world – where the Logos is terribly inverted, thrown, fallen and at a loss – it's no wonder that paradox, chiliasm, chiasmus, dialectics, inversion, subversion, re-version, become ways, after Hacker, of reading and atoning for that very world's ill logic.

Alex Niven, chosen young essayist

Bunting's Persia: Translations by Basil Bunting ed. Don Share
(Chicago: Flood Editions, 2012).

In January 1935, Basil Bunting wrote to Ezra Pound from his temporary home in the Canary Islands. Bunting was engaged in a translation of the Persian epic, Ferdowsi's *Shahnameh*, which he had first encountered while he was living with Pound in the Italian town of Rapallo in the early thirties. In Rapallo, Pound had been enthused by the idea of an English translation. So Bunting was piqued when he received a postcard from Pound saying he could now see little value in the project. Bunting's riposte is interesting enough to be quoted at length:

> I think you, as you would, hit on the main difficulty of epic poetry in this age, without being possibly quite aware of it or its implications. You say all F[erdowsi]'s characters (as portrayed by me) bore you. It hadn't occurred to me that you would think first of the characters, nevertheless I now see you would. But in trying to learn something about epic I was very largely trying to get away from characters and deal with acts instead ...
>
> It is true that Firdusi's [sic] people talk more than Homer's, and write letters, and in the Persian, at least, they do have 'characters' of a simple sort (and convincing sort), but what is important is still the act, and the letters are themselves acts, not in the least 'arranged' to display character ...
>
> It occurred to me a long time ago that this indirect business had gone about as far as it would go without degenerating. Nobody is going to do it better than you for a hell of a long time, and [Louis] Zuk[ofsky] can only introduce further complications of method that remove it from the possible reader, step by step, until somebody will arise who will justify the kind of things the academic nincompoops used to say about you, and be totally unintelligible ... I can do nothing with it that will satisfy me. It is much better to leave the field to you, and perhaps to Zuk's elaborations and try telling a story...[1]

This was more than a personal quarrel, more than cavilling. Translating

---

[1] Basil Bunting, letter to Ezra Pound, 4 January 1935, Beinecke Rare Book and Manuscript Library, Yale University (New Haven, Conn.).

Ferdowsi appeared to offer Bunting an escape route from what he calls here 'this indirect business' – the emphasis on psychological inwardness that had in his view led modern poetry into a cul-de-sac by the mid 1930s. At this point there was much need of a new departure of this kind. When Bunting remarked to Pound that he could 'do nothing with it' that would satisfy him, he was talking about modernist poetry as a whole. After leaving the 'Ezuversity' of Rapallo in 1933, Bunting's own creativity had stalled. By the mid-thirties, he was producing very little original verse, and the wider milieu that had sustained him in the first years of the decade was beginning to falter. The initial excitement that had greeted the publication of the 'Objectivist" issue of *Poetry* (Chicago) in February 1931 – an inauguration event for second wave modernists like Bunting, George Oppen, Charles Reznikoff, and Louis Zukofsky – had dissipated in this era of Depression and exile. Eliot was writing plays and priggish literary criticism. Pound's *Cantos* were degenerating into their own indirect business of fascism, economic cant and prose collages. Something had to give, and for Bunting the answer lay in the combination of action and epic narrative he found in the *Shahnameh*.

Unfortunately, this particular escape route from modernist impasse was never tested. Bunting's application for a Guggenheim had already fallen through by the time of the letter to Pound. In the difficult climate of the period, Bunting was unable to rein in modernist 'unintelligibility' by learning from the Persian past. Dejected and without a publisher, by the end of the thirties he had abandoned poetry altogether for an improbable existence working as a sailor on transatlantic ships. Not until his famous revival in the 1960s would he give voice to his own late-modernist 'story', the autobiographical mini-epic *Briggflatts* (1966).

But by that stage Bunting's interest in Persia had long since become a cornerstone of his life and art in ways he could not have envisaged in 1935. During World War II his knowledge of ancient Persian was the springboard for a momentous real-life relationship: Bunting spent much of the war and some of the ensuing peace in Tehran, working successively as an R.A.F. officer, an M.I.6. agent, and a *London Times* journalist, before returning to the UK in 1951 accompanied by a young Persian wife, Sima Alladadian. *The Spoils*, a long 'sonata poem' published in *Poetry* in 1951, condensed much of Bunting's experience of Persia and its literature into original verse. However, the *Shahnameh* project would remain unfinished and largely unpublished for the remainder of Bunting's life. Fragments appeared in collected editions of Bunting from the early fifties onwards, as did renderings of other Persian poets such as Sa'di and Manuchehri, but they remained scattered curiosities.

We are fortunate then, that Bunting's Persian experiments have now been brought together in a more-or-less comprehensive format. Don Share, whose long-awaited critical edition of Bunting's poems is forthcoming from Faber, has assembled a well presented, neatly arranged book that collates some twenty Persian translations grouped chronologically in sequence of the original authors (Rudaki, Ferdowsi, Manuchehri, Sa'di, Hafez, and Obaid-e Zakani). There is also a glossary, biographies of the poets, and a useful introduction

The resulting anthology is slight for all its exhaustiveness, and there is understandably little connective tissue between many of the fragments. Half a millennium separates the birth of the earliest poet here, Abu Abdollah Ja'far ibn Mohammad Rudaki (ca 859-940), from the death of the latest, Khajeh Shams al-Din Mohammad Hafez (ca 1315-1390), which is roughly the interval between Chaucer and Tennyson. We should therefore be wary of treating 'Bunting's Persia' as a unified entity. The collection begins with a typically Bunting-esque statement of world-weariness – Rudaki's 'All the teeth ever I had are worn down and fallen out' – but it ends with a comic poem in rhyming couplets, Obaid e-Zakani's *The Pious Cat*. While it certainly stands as evidence of Bunting's desire to tell stories, this anthology should not be interpreted as a précis of a great thirties epic that never was. In fact it is an appropriately piebald compendium for a writer who felt he only discovered his true poetic voice with the publication of *Briggflatts* late in life.

For all that, there are several moments here where it is possible to detect Bunting's style establishing itself, as it both reconstitutes and learns from the Persian source material. This is observable in another extract from the opening, untitled translation of Rudaki:

The world is always like a round, rolling eye,
round and rolling since it existed: a cure for pain
and then again a pain that supplants the cure.
In a certain time it makes new things old,
in a certain time makes new what has been threadbare.
Many a broken desert has been a gay garden,
many gay gardens grow where there used to be a desert.

Bunting's elegiac style, which drew equally on Pound at his most deadpan and macabre (especially the sixth section of *Propertius*) and on the scepticism of a northern Quaker background, has found its métier here in this hymn to a circular determinism. 'A cure for pain and then again a pain that supplants the cure'. There can few more fitting epigraphs for Bunting's worldview anywhere in his oeuvre.

Whether his interpretation of it was correct or not, it seems that the discovery of the Persian canon allowed Bunting to indulge his fondness for the fatalistic, the foreboding, the stoical. He continued to emphasise the lugubrious mode he had established in works such as *Villon* (1925) and *Chomei at Toyama* (1933), while also laying the foundations for lines such as the Coda to *Briggflatts* ('Blind, we follow / rain slant, spray flick / in fields we do not know') and the famous opening of *The Spoils*:

Man's life so little worth,
Do we fear to take or lose it?
No ill companion on a journey, Death
lays his purse on the table and opens the wine.

Indeed, it is difficult to imagine that a work like *The Spoils* wasn't in some way influenced by Bunting's readings of Ferdowsi, which engendered translations like the following attempt at a passage from the *Shahnameh*:

When the sword of sixty comes nigh his head
give a man no wine, for he is drunk with years.
Age claps a stick in my bridle-hand ...

Such prototypical sources are immensely useful, and anyone interested in joining the dots in Bunting's creative evolution will be grateful for Share's edition. Most helpfully, it provides a handy survey of Bunting's development in the thirty-year lean period between the mid thirties and the mid sixties, a period from which the vast majority of these translations date.

Countless aspects of Bunting's Persia remain unexplored, partly because the critical canon on Bunting is still relatively meagre. Despite a moderate upsurge in interest in recent years (a new Bloodaxe edition of *Briggflatts* published in 2009, a small conference at the University of Durham in 2012) he is not a fashionable figure, particularly in the UK where the Bloomsbury version of modernism Bunting loathed is now more popular than ever. As such, this new collection has arrived at a good moment to initiate a critical discussion about a fascinating and bizarrely neglected topic.

There are signs that Persian poetry is beginning to make inroads into an Anglophone readership. In 2012, *Six Vowels and Twenty-three Consonants*, an anthology of Persian poetry edited and translated by Ali Alizadeh and John Kinsella, proved that the vibrant tradition of Ferdowsi and Hafez extends into the present (the youngest poet in the collection, Ahmad Zahedi Langroodi, was born in 1982). Hopefully, projects like *Six Vowels* – which is as accessible as it is educative – will be the prelude to a wider opening up of dialogues between Persian and Anglophone verse cultures. Granting more centrality to Basil Bunting's lifelong engagement with Persia could help to redraw the map of modern poetry in this way. At a time when research into both modernism and global literatures is such a massive worldwide industry, the example of a colleague of Pound and Yeats who departed into ancient Persia in his creative life and the contemporary Middle East in actuality is surely a compelling subject for research. What was the real nature of Bunting's relationship with Persia? Given that his professional role there in World War II was as an officer in an Imperial regime, is his poetic engagement with Persian literature a more complicated matter than might first appear? Might Bunting's readings of Persian poets have prepared the way for his most notable late-modernist innovations? For now we can enjoy the often exquisitely wrought poetry in this beautiful, judiciously edited book, but hopefully some interesting debates about Bunting's Persia will commence in the wake of its publication.

CHOSEN BROADSHEET POETS

Simon Kohli is twenty-nine years of age. He currently lives and works in Greater London. His poems have appeared in *Agenda* Broadsheet 18.

Cryonics

Anna wears the rain
like jewels in her hair

as she moves across
Siberia's itchy spine

and over a rank skin
of history, the exiled bones

of old-time crooks
and rebels; past the gap-tooth greeting of a crone

clinging to radioactive cabbages.
Anna's drawn to these abandoned places

where soils groan their sickness
and a phantom up-the-nostrils

brings surface to the half conserved-in
brain-juice and bio-electrics

of *bygone   bygone   bygones*
and oil-streaked overalls

sweat-worn,
scrunched in suds.

Spring air: clean.

The harsh cry of a bedraggled fox
brings her back to earth

and she sees the buildings
in the same light

as she did thirty years ago:
functional and grey.

But now the old block is an urn
for the ashes of yesterday

in a district so empty
not even the hard slap of a footstep echoes.

She stops on the pavement.
Saturates herself in the unseen twinkle
        of a mammoth winking

from its frozen depth,
an epoch

        preserved in rain that killed the geiger needle;
in splinters of ozone; in the juice of a deathcap ...

The undegradable duffle coat and the broken lift.

The elderly neighbour that beat his own brain
in a vodka game
a red ghost on dull cement.

Anna dismisses them
and ventures upstairs to the third floor

where number seventy-six beckons her
with a pristine sheen

that flips the heart.
An eye clutches at dimness –

a mockery of dentures
clench in their sockets –

a coarse hand trembles – a freckled key slots
in, and with a clockwise twist

the red door smoothes ajar
and she's back in the old living room

where nothing had encroached –
no cobwebs, no patches of mould,
no rags of moss, nor any other green reclaimer.

Through a curtain crack a beam
gives her face a touch of frost

and the spirit of the place offers her
       an old settee

where she sits a-crackle –
back-straight, hand-on-knee
like something of quick-freeze

arrived: she moves no more.

Sarah Sibley is 27 and works for a small publisher in the Suffolk countryside. She has a BA in Creative Writing and Literary Studies from Wolverhampton University and last year completed her MA with distinction at Lancaster University. She previously featured in Broadsheet 15 and elsewhere has been published in *Orbis, Obsessed with Pipework* , *The Delinquent* and *The Interpreter's house*.

Lone Man Stories

Up at High Winds farm by the slurry pit
we'd hide and seek in a thicket
ripped every night by storms –
the kind we don't get in these parts anymore.
For a time, stories of a lone man
wiped us out from the copse.
Rik Loader said he'd crossed back in,
showed us his souvenir – a knife,
its blade the width of my thigh.

At night I dreamt of the thicket;
in my hiding place a dead fox,
the lone man lost in a cloud of gnats.
Another time, the startled pigs
and spooked horses tipped his mind
and he went staggering into the pit;
at the farm a single light kept vigil –
no stir from the brush,
a campfire burned to dust.

After he died

she walked barefoot in the snow,
slept with every window open
inviting a coldness to match her own.

The invasions of her silent world –
every plane overhead,
she disconnects the telephone.

Knitting through the slow hours;
small movements scarcely keeping her together.
His song blaring from a car on the road
or a voice like his on the radio
unravels her constrain.

In the laundry basket, his clothes.
Legs and arms dance on the washing line
all through the night; in her dream they float
to the depths of the garden
no sunlight ever raising them from shadow.

Ship Desk

I could have been flung overboard with smoke floats,
not detained at port without explanation.
I imagine the bottom of the ocean,
the torment of long arms tugging on nestled drawers;
a giant octopus swimming off with a cluster of my mahogany boxes
while plankton swish through keyholes.

On solid ground, there's not the comforting creak of the ship's bowels
but they found me a relative's house
that likes to stretch its oak beams and wooden floors.
I'm not your great granddad's anymore.
I'm for phonebooks, the bank folder, the hole punch.
I smell of absent keys and warm money
not of salt and sweat and changeable weather that you'd expect.

The Visitant

The mariner tells me he wasn't supposed to die,
that graveyards just aren't him.
He's brought a sickly floral smell indoors;
for weeks I'm scared of sweet peas, carnations, lilies.

I can only get shipping forecasts on the radio now
and he makes himself at home whenever I go away –
I shake sand from bed sheets,
wash the brine off the settee.

Death never looks for his strays
so today I stood in the garden pond
and guided the mariner back to the other side –
my trousers rolled up, an anchor attached to my ankle.

The Widower

Outside, trees creep closer and closer
to scratch and poke broken panes,
an east wind pitches to the frame.
He blocks the howling with an old Free Press,
draws green curtains, thicket heavy.
In the mirror he is unkempt,
face pecked by sorrow.
On the phone, words catch in his throat,
crackle for life then die.

Upstairs a thimble mutters to itself
under her old dressing table.
He takes her blanket from the cedarwood chest,
throws a dead spider from her favourite Doulton teacup.
All merriment blown down the chimney from distant homes
snags on exposed carpet tacks
then folds in his lap.

Nicola Lewis was born in Cardiff in 1987. She studied English Literature at Cardiff University and graduated in 2008. She writes poetry and short stories and has previously had the poem 'Redundant' chosen in Broadsheet 11 of *Agenda*.

The House

They spend their evenings divided by a flight of stairs;
the TVs do the talking, filling the house with unnatural noise.

Every room feels too warm, the air dense.
The vase harbours spiders in the dark of the cupboard,
the recycling bins clink with empty bottles.

The perfume he bought on a weekend away has not been used for weeks,
she does not want the scent on her body.
The silver bracelet lies undisturbed in the jewellery box:
she likes the breeze and space around her wrist.

Neither of them sleep very well.
They are too aware of the body that lies beside them.

Each day, she steps out of the house and into the light.
She shuts the door tightly, locking the stench of dying inside.

NOTES FOR BROADSHEET POETS

Trees against the sky: the poetry of **Felix Dennis**
by **Alison Brackenbury**

Do all poetry readings need hushed quiet? Are all modern poems dogged by a sense of difficulty? No. This was brought home to me by a performance on a wet autumn evening, two years ago.

The (paying) audience was rumbustious. A writer whispered to me that she had never seen any of them before at any local poetry event. I had never seen a poetry reading attended by so many young men. This was a new audience, not unlike a noisy works dinner. Felix Dennis arrived in front of them to deliver his poems. The performance was immaculately choreographed. The strongly rhymed poems were, by turns, funny, rude, and moving. The audience loved them. So did I.

I first struggled to understand the nature of criticism as a confused undergraduate at Oxford. My subsequent First is, I am afraid, proof of youthful bluff rather than mature academic solidity. Academe and I parted company with mutual relief. For the next thirty years, I continued to observe the exercise of critical judgement, whether nervously reading reviews of my own poems, or, still more nervously, standing by flimsy ropes at horse shows, as Welsh cobs thudded past. During the last ten years I have become a writer of reviews: a role for which nobody is fully qualified. From all this, (and some interesting times on judging panels), I have concluded that once a type of poetry, (or cob), is defined and accepted, it is relatively easy to agree on the worst and best examples. The really ferocious fights are about which types should be valued. (Never ask a breeder of pedigree dogs about Labradoodles...)

Where would I place Felix Dennis' work? In a ring for particularly bright-eyed beasts, clumsily labelled 'popular poetry'. Breed characteristics: appears simple (which masks much skill); appeals to an audience who may not have read or studied poetry in depth (proved, in Dennis' case, by his own performances). May be funny. Often uses traditional forms, especially rhymed. I strongly approve of popular poetry, although I consider a couple of its most successful practitioners to be lightweight and unconvincing. These do not include Felix Dennis.

Dennis, who began to write poetry in his fifties, is a prolific producer of very varied poems. This creates an immediate critical problem (which I also labour under). The work of a prolific poet is almost always labelled 'uneven'. No doubt some poems are published too soon. But I think this can be a mistaken reaction to the range of the work within one collection. The critic's problem is the reader's gain. There is more likely to be a poem which will appeal to a particular reader than in a slimmer, more 'even' collection. Frequent writing can also strengthen technique, so that a poem's energy does not depend merely on a sense of the poet's self or subject, but on a firm understanding of patterning within a line or stanza.

Dennis' poems have strong bones. His best couplets are brisk, with the bite of epigram: 'More lame in the world than ride.' ('More') He is an accomplished writer of ballads, whether in the familiar abab stanza or in couplets (aabb), both forms known to John Clare. The last two lines of Clare's terrifying poem 'The Badger' hold echoes from – interestingly – a humorous ballad starring 'The Dragon of Ware'. With or without its dragons, the ballad is a testing form, as the second and last lines of each stanza are often shortened. Poets must, in the end, know where they are going. Dennis does:

> More tears are shed for answered prayers
> Than ever those refused.
>> ('The Wishing Tree')

Most of Dennis' poems are in such short, lively forms. But he can also tease meaning through longer stanzas, with some striking variants, such as the poem in five-line stanzas (abbba) which ends, unexpectedly, with an isolated line which repeats the poem's opening: 'I want to plant a walnut wood.' ('The Walnut Wood')

Dennis' range is shown clearly in poems of the natural world. He can evoke the exotic white cedar:

> The leaves are leather discs; they scud and scrape
> Along a shingled roof at night like claws.
>> ('Ba-ma-ta')

The poem's loving precision is reserved for a species which 'except for tree-lovers, is not perhaps, a thing of beauty'. Dennis owns the cedar, but his poetry shows an unusual awareness of the limits of possession. 'Arrival of the New Owner' describes an imagined meeting with two estate workers, gamekeepers (like my grandfather): 'The land was theirs. And remained theirs, still.' He can view farmland as a productive workplace, with its own exact language: 'Silage spilling from the clamp'. ('Autumn Harvest'). But Dennis also understands the world (as, I fear, some farmers no longer do) as a living web, with many inhabitants. This is not a sentimental vision. Grass may be 'To us a lawn – to hens, a killing ground.' ('All Nature's Art'). Worse still, the monoculture of the lawn is, for insects, 'A dreary harsh savanna', the tiny reflection of a devastated world.

As the world outside poetry is in very bad shape, I think it should be mentioned that, thanks to Dennis, 100,000 native broadleaf trees are planted in Britain each year. Only 10% of British land is covered by forest. The average for the rest of Europe is 37%. I was born in the north of Lincolnshire, whose great fields were left treeless by modern agriculture. But landowners preserved small areas of woodland for their own pleasures. Through accidents of employment, both my father and I spent part of our childhoods finding owls, robins' nests and the white stars of anemones, marooned upon the wooded islands of the rich. Dennis is trying to connect these islands.

But the tree-planter grew up in London. Dennis can summon up his city with a vicious verve – and knowing slang – as sharp as an eighteenth century ballad:

Downstairs, the foxes dance on chairs
While bouncers strip the marks.

'In a Soho Garden', the 'foxes' are prostitutes, the 'marks', their gullible victims, lured into den-like clubs. In 'Armoured in Innocence', the past shouts from the page, in the staccato chants of anti-war demos: 'Hey! Hey! LBJ! How many kids did you bomb today?' More lightly, 'Snakeskin Boots' restores London in 1964, a girl and 'my snakeskin boots with their Cuban heel'.

One of cold-hearted art's warmest gifts is to enlarge experience. One of the fascinations of Guy Garvey's award-winning songs for his group, Elbow, is his account of male friendship, drinking, and his street memories as a boy. Reading Dennis' poems – and his excellent notes – I am equally fascinated to see that, as well as the sex, he remembers his clothes: 'a full length military cloak and chiffon scarf'... 'Build a rocket, boys', Garvey sings hopefully. Dennis' companions too have 'rocket-ships', but, more brutally, boyhood is the time when ties become 'garrotting cords'. ('When')

The shocking twist – the flick of poetry's wrist – is a particular gift of Dennis. It can flash out in a phrase: 'the bailiff, Love'. ('Grief seeks Loss'). A mellow account of England's past suddenly suggests

And foxes sought out Squire's pack
To race them for the thrill.
                    ('An Older England')

166

Reliable, but unattributable sources tell me that the darker woods of the Cotswolds still offer this exciting chance, every autumn, to fox cubs. They don't seem to get very far. Perhaps some forthcoming prosecutions will slip past the encircling hounds.

Robert Frost, by all accounts a terrible farmer, wisely probed the farming proverb: 'Good fences make good neighbours'. Dennis' poem on boundaries turns to searing honesty: 'Our lives are warped by property [...] A wall brings out the worst in men'. ('Of Walls and Fences') Even the boundaries of life are dissolved by a doctor's account of near-death: 'You wandered through an open door'. ('Life Support')

As energetic performance demonstrates, sound is the open door into Dennis' poetry. He recollects being 'hooked' into poetry by his teacher reading – aloud – 'The Charge of the Light Brigade'. ('The Ballad of "Abdul" Rowe'). But what are the barriers to critical acceptance of his own work?

I think there are two problematic qualities in Dennis' style. One – which I share – is the distortion of normal syntax to fit metre and rhyme. Poetry is unforgiving of shortcuts. Poets must be, too. The second is his occasional use of archaic, consciously 'poetic' language. In 'April 15' Dennis' adored cherry tree is called a 'white-lipped maiden'. 'White-lipped' is, I think, excellent, but 'maiden' reads as a lazy nod to the past. The tree is lost. Housman – just – successfully introduces 'maiden' into one of his most beautiful lyrics: 'With rue my heart is laden'. But the poem ends with 'rose-lipped girls'. No one can tone and shade a poem more finely than Housman. Listen to the master. If the 'white-lipped maiden' became a girl, the cherry tree would spring back into the poem.

Cherries figure in one of my three favourite poems by Dennis. But the first of his poems which I read celebrates a different tree: the hornbeam. It was in a free pamphlet from the excellent charity, Poems in the Waiting Room, that I found 'The Hornbeams'. A London policeman is puzzled to find Dennis gazing up, then, in turn, is struck by admiration:

A man entranced beneath a tree
His head bent back, yet strangely bare,
His helmet doffed –

Why does this strangely bare narrative work? I think it draws on the power of exact naming, and of knowledge. How many poets could recognise the pattern of hornbeam twigs against the sky? I certainly could not.

I can recognise, approvingly, the four-line stanza of the bluntly titled 'Going Bald', with a multi-syllable rhyme followed by a single rhyming syllable; an eleven-syllable line followed by one of ten. This is the stanza of 'If', by Kipling. I have written admiringly elsewhere about Kipling. His poems are a savage reproach to our own politicians' lack of understanding of Afghanistan, whose invaders die 'Shot like a rabbit in a ride'. Dennis inherits Kipling's plain-speaking, to different ends. In 'Going Bald', he is a lyric poet, whose grasp of strict form brings out a mordant elegance: 'And winter finds us out, and death persuades us'.

I am completely persuaded by the third, and last, of my favourite poems by Dennis: 'I Plucked all the Cherries'. It is untouched by archaic diction or twisted syntax. Its simplicity is charged by a lifetime's experience: 'Done with the getting of / What I could get'. Driven by rhythm, ringing with rhyme, its lines offer many gifts: 'Take them and welcome – / I'm done with them now'. I hope Dennis will write more of these bare, urgent poems.

Although his poetry is highly entertaining, on and off the page, Dennis' own notes to his work do not claim that poems exist to amuse or console. 'Poetry' he writes, 'cauterises the wound of life'. It is a good metaphor. Its truth – for I must believe that poetry deals with truth – is vivid in the work of Felix Dennis. For the emerging writer, Dennis' poems stand as a heartening reminder that British poetry today is a wood with many paths.

Martyn Crucefix

Microautobiograph

August 1974 – August 1975

The makings of a writer

i

It was August and as I walked from the red-roofed, Wiltshire house where I'd lived most of my 18 years, I had a vision of a child, a baby staring up at me, waiting to be lifted. It lasted only a few seconds but I returned to the house happier and resolved that I could not turn my back on such an opportunity.

I'd applied to study Medicine for reasons I cannot now recover and may not have been clear at the time. I'd had a series of interviews during the Upper Sixth year but only rejections had come back though I was held on a short list at Guys in London. But I'd already been struggling to focus on Biology, Chemistry and Physics, preferring to pick up the blonde, resonant body of my guitar and play Neil Young, Bowie, Lindisfarne, Don Maclean's *American Pie*. I had written a few poems but from an almost complete ignorance of poetry. Shakespeare and Chaucer at O-level really was about it. My models were exclusively song lyrics which I listened to intensely, following them on the lyric sheets inside the unfolding gates of album covers. My head was unhelpfully full of phrases from Van der Graaf Generator's *Peter Hammill* and Jon Anderson of Yes – one a merchant of genuine, existential, gothic angst, the other a lyrical fantasist. Then Guys rang to offer me a reserve place to start in ten days time. Then came the vision of the child.

ii

Because of the lateness of the arrangements in getting to London, I lodged in a room in Eltham Park and commuted into London Bridge. The city I'd been parachuted into was in the midst of the Provisional IRA bombing campaign. The medical school worked us hard though I never found it easy, or easy to devote myself to it. Within a week or so, we filed into the long upper room overlooking the inner quad. The windows down one side were filled with pallid light, a cloud-light flooding in from the London morning. We had watched a film which included queasy moments of blades easing through human skin though even as I watched, it struck me as less informative, more likely to be readying us for the shock of encountering our first lifeless body.

His head was to the pale light of the morning. His feet were dry and yellowy and up-turned from the horizontal table where he lay. Though he'd once been human, he hardly seemed to be any longer. His skin was tough and thick-seeming, exactly like leather. The mound of a belly rose and fell to his groin dusted with greying pubic hair, a shrivelled prick and half-hidden balls. His legs ran on, thin and bony at the knee down to the up-turned toes. We all avoided looking at his face.

I wish I could remember who made the first cut. One of us must have done: into the leathery skin above the sternum. The blade needed pressing firmly and the upper layers peeled open a bit like a zip fastener, down towards the abdomen. We did not give him a name though we turned up to visit him every week for the rest of term. But then, he wasn't ours alone. As we gradually opened up thorax and abdomen, arms and legs, students in the year above us were coming at other times and we'd arrive to find his skull opened, his cheeks slipping down his face, his eyes suddenly gaping and exposed to the light that greyed and wizened as the winter term progressed.

iii

By November, I'd already bolted back to Wiltshire a couple of times and instead of medical text books, I'd started reading Hardy, Lawrence and H.E. Bates. In a poignant reminder of happier times, the school asked me to choose my books for a prize-giving at Christmas. On a trip to Bath, I bought Graham Greene's *The End of the Affair*, Leonard Cohen's *Beautiful Losers* and Lawrence's *England, My England*. In Trowbridge, I scoured the second-hand bookshelves of Newbury's, a bric-à-brac shop long since demolished and one morning I found a copy of George Eliot's *Silas Marner* and a book called *The Manifold and the One* by Agnes Arber. I knew nothing of the latter but must have been attracted to the philosophical sounding title. In my growing tribulations at Guys, I was becoming deep. The questions I seemed to ask myself more and more had no easy answers and I had a notion this was called philosophy.

The Arber book was a wide-ranging and syncretic survey, drawing on literary, scientific, religious, mystical and philosophical traditions, in pursuit of the experience which Arber defines as 'that direct and unmediated contemplation which is characterised by a peculiarly intense awareness of a Whole as the Unity of all things'. Amidst the dissections, test tubes, bunsens, the red- and blue-dyed lung trees and chemical equations with which I uneasily engaged back in Southwark, I found consolation in Arber's idea that life is an imperfect struggle. In those winter months, failing to work hard enough or get a firm footing in the bewildering city, I did not read passages about the 'inevitable appearance of the awry and the fragmentary which we isolate in our minds' in a very philosophical fashion. Rather this was my daily diet, strap-hanging on a delayed train into London Bridge, sneaking into emergency exits to catch the second half of Diana Rigg in *Pygmalion* on St Martin's Lane, trudging up a drizzly Charing Cross Road to buy sheet music I could not afford, drinking with others in The Bunch of Grapes on St Thomas Street, complaining how much work I had yet to do.

Already letters to old school friends were raising the prospect of leaving medical school. When Arber wrote of the limited and artificial confinement of conventional thought ('a hard and fast orthodox system of logical regulations – many of which resemble the rules of a complicated game and have little concern with the attainment of truth'), I felt she was talking of my current studies. I had developed an attraction to the esoteric – it made me feel more justifiably the outsider that I felt myself to be – and I got untold pleasure from hearing that masters of Zen Buddhism might declare to my lecturers, 'Supreme Enlightenment goes beyond the narrow range of intellection – Cease from measuring heaven with a tiny piece of reed'.

iv

But work piled up rapidly in the new term and after renewed attempts to devote myself to it, still the old patterns of neglect and procrastination returned. Even though there were months left before I managed to act on my desire to leave Guys, to beat a retreat from the big city, to set a new and more deliberate course, still the length of remembered time now seems short. After Lawrence's *Apocalypse* and Sartre's *The Age of Reason*, I raced through Cohen's *Beautiful Losers*, bewildered by its episodic narrative, its explicit sexuality. It was Arber's utterly different book that haunted me. One evening, staring out at Eltham, I wrote: 'Down in the street / the puddles turn to raging light / night-time folds away the day / packing up the sun. Turning / through the broken stars, over, under / the chosen Far, making for homeward'. I listened to Radio Caroline in the evenings when I'd managed – not always and increasingly less often – a couple of hours of legitimate work.

Then travelling blearily east from London Bridge, I forgot to grab my briefcase before stepping down onto the platform. It was a self-inflicted injury but had little real influence on the string of failures I achieved in the final exams. On another day – this was my nineteenth birthday – Margaret Thatcher defeated Ted Heath for the Conservative leadership. One day

– it was a Friday – a train from Drayton Park failed to stop at Moorgate, overshooting the platform into a dead-end tunnel at 8.46 in the morning. As I walked gloomily from London Bridge through the black, wrought-iron gates of Guys, forty-three people were killed.

One morning three months later, I found myself sitting in the room in Crookston Road, the noise of the busy A2 a distant growling. I stared at my packed bags and felt calm if utterly becalmed. One day, months later again – this was now the end of a second strangely untethered summer – the thought had begun to form that I might see myself as a student of philosophy, maybe work harder at the writing.

Colin Wilcockson

Northwick Lodge, Harrow-on-the-Hill: David Jones's Residence for 17 Years

David Jones outside Northwick Lodge.

From 1947 to 1964 David Jones lived in Northwick Lodge, a house owned by Harrow School, at the foot of the hill. It was used as an overspill by the school, and was managed by Christopher Carlile, a retired member of the teaching staff. I lived there from January to April 1955 during the practical term of my studying for the University of Oxford Post-graduate Diploma in Education, as did two other intending teachers on the same course. The remaining rooms were rented by a variety of people who wanted board and lodging. A married couple living in the basement did the cooking and cleaning. I seem to recall that there were some ten or a dozen of us at the evening dinners, presided iover by Christopher, a kind and gentle person.

For much of my stay, I spent the evenings after dinner in David Jones's room, where we discussed language and literature and art and matters Welsh, and drank Earl Gray tea. Needless to say, I had a lot more to learn from him that he from me: at that time there was an exhibition of David's work at The Tate Gallery, and he had published *In Parenthesis* in 1937 and *The Anathemata*

173

in 1952. David loved the room he had at Northwick Lodge, where so much of his most productive work was done, including some of his best known paintings.[1] The room was at the back of the house and overlooked the school playing fields. I recall his remarking how much the brightly coloured football shirts of the teams pleased him. But in 1964 a decision was made to demolish the house. In a letter to me dated Sat-Sun, March 7th-8th, 1964, the opening sentence reads: 'Thank you so much for yr letter. This is but a brief note of reply because I am in the most ghastly mess – with some suddenness the house is being closed down & I'm in the chaos of trying to deal with 14 [actually 17] years accumulation of stuff in this one beloved room.' He was always saddened by the loss. Two years later, in a letter dated 3rd January, 1966, written from Monksdene Hotel, he writes, 'I sadly miss being up at Northwick Lodge in my high room – but the house closed down , & now it has been pulled down so you would not know it had ever been there.'

Photographs of David in his 'high room' have been reproduced, but I think none exists of the exterior, giving some impression of the style of the conventionally Victorian Northwick Lodge. I here reproduce a snapshot (unfortunately partly occupied by myself) because it is the only extant record of the house in which David Jones spent some of his most creative years.

---

[1] For a chronological list of David Jones' paintings, see Nicolete Gray, *The Paintings of David Jones*, Hatfield and London, in association with the Tate Gallery, 1989, pp.6-7.

Biographies

Josephine Balmer's collections and translations include *The Word for Sorrow* (Salt, 2009), *Chasing Catullus: Poems, Translations and Transgressions* (Bloodaxe, 2004), *Catullus: Poems of Love and Hate* (Bloodaxe, 2004), *Classical Women Poets* (Bloodaxe, 1996) and *Sappho: Poems & Fragments* (Bloodaxe, 1992). She has written widely on poetry and translation for publications such as the *Observer*, the *Independent on Sunday*, the *Times Literary Supplement* and the *New Statesman*, and currently reviews poetry for the *Times*. Her study of classical translation and poetic versioning, *Piecing Together the Fragments*, will be published by OUP in 2013.

William Bedford is an award-winning novelist, children's novelist, poet and short-story writer, his work appearing in magazines around the world. His novel *Happiland* was shortlisted for the *Guardian* Fiction Prize. His selected poems, *Collecting Bottle Tops*, and selected short stories and non-fiction, *None of the Cadillacs Was Pink*, were both published in 2009.

Khayke Beruriah Wiegand is a Yiddish poet and academic living in London, where she teaches Yiddish language and literature and is very active in a reviving culture. She also teaches at the Yiddish Studies Centre in Oxford and has given academic papers throughout Europe and in New York. A bilingual book of her own poetry *Have You Seen My Goat? And Other Poems* was published in Tel Aviv in 2011 and her work has also appeared in the bilingual anthology *Step By Step : Contemporary Yiddish Poetry* (2009). She co-translated, together with Stephen Watts, A. N. Stencl's *All My Young Years* (Five Leaves 2007) and a second selection of their translations of Stencl's later poetry awaits publication.

Marina Boroditskaya is an acclaimed poet, translator and children's author. She has published many English works in Russian translation, including Chaucer's *Troilus and Criseyde*, Browning, Burns, Stevenson, the poets of the Silver Age, *The Gruffalo* and most recently *The Comedy of Errors*. She has published five collections of poetry, the most recent of which is *An Ode to Shortsightedness*. She is well-loved across Russia for her lyrical and witty children's stories and rhymes.

Alison Brackenbury was born in 1953. Her eighth collection, *Now and Then*, was published in April 2013 by Carcanet. New poems can be seen at her website: www.alisonbrackenbury.co.uk .

Marga Burgui-Artajo is a linguist and translator. Born on the edges of Spain and Catalunya she has lived in London for many years. With Stephen Watts she is translating the poetry of Adnan al-Sayegh into English: *The Deleted Part* (Exiled Writers Ink 2009), and the long poem *Pages From the Biography Of An Exile*. A full collection in translation is awaiting publication. She is also translating the Catalan poet Victor Sunyol and immersing herself in the language & culture of Scots Gaelic.

For some years **Ruth Christie** has been translating from the fiction, poetry and prose of Turkish literature. Recent work has focused on the poetry of the Kurdish woman poet Bejan Matur. The translations, in collaboration with Selçuk Berilgen, of her latest work of poems, *How Abraham Abandoned Me* has been published by Arc in 2012 and awarded the Spring Recommended Translation by the P.B.S.

Caroline Clark's first collection *Saying Yes in Russian* was published by Agenda Editions in 2012. She comes from Lewes and currently lives in Montreal.

Belinda Cooke teaches English in the Highlands. Her Russian translations, poetry and reviews have been published widely. A chapbook came out in 2008 and her first full-length collection of translations, *Paths of the Beggarwoman: The Selected Poems of Marina Tsvetaeva*, was published by the Worple Press also in 2008. In collaboration with Richard McKane, she has also published a translation of Boris Poplavsky's *Flags* (Shearsman Press, 2010).

David Cooke won a Gregory Award in 1977 and published his first collection, *Brueghel's Dancers* in 1984. His retrospective collection, *In the Distance*, was published in 2011 by Night Publishing and a collection of more recent pieces, *Work Horses*, has recently been published by Ward Wood Publishing. His poems, translations and reviews have appeared widely in journals.

Martyn Crucefix has won numerous prizes including a major Eric Gregory award and a Hawthornden Fellowship. He has published 5 collections, including *An English Nazareth* (Enitharmon, 2004) and *Hurt* (Enitharmon, 2010). His translation of Rilke's *Duino Elegies* was shortlisted for the 2007 Popescu Prize for European Poetry Translation and hailed as "unlikely to be bettered for very many years" (Magma). His translation of Rilke's *Sonnets to Orpheus* is due Autumn 2012.

Peter Dale's most recent publications are *Peter Dale in Conversation with Cynthia Haven*, published by Between the Lines Press, *Under the Breath*, poems, and *Wry-Blue Loves,* a verse translation of Tristan Corbière, which received a Poetry Book Society Recommendation for Translation – both published by Anvil Press Poetry, as is his terza rima translation of *The Divine Comedy*, now going into its seventh edition. His translation of Paul Valéry, *Charms and Other Pieces*, Anvil, appeared in 2007 and is now in its second edition. His current book of verse is the sequence *Local Habitation,* 2009, also from Anvil who will publish his new book, *Diffractions: New and Collected Poems* in spring 2012. He now lives in Cardiff.

Greg Delanty's latest book of poems is *The Greek Anthology, Book XVII*, Carcanet Press. Other recent books are *Loosestrife*, Fomite Press; *The Word Exchange, Anglo-Saxon Poems in Translation*, WW Norton; and his *Collected Poems 1986-2006*, Carcanet Press. He has received many awards, most recently a Guggenheim for poetry. He teaches at Saint Michael's College, Vermont.

Jordi Doce (Gijón, Spain, 1967) holds a BA in English Literature and wrote a M. Phil Thesis on the work of Peter Redgrove. He worked as Language Assistant at The University of Oxford (1997-2000) and has translated into Spanish the poetry of T.S. Eliot, W. H. Auden, Charles Tomlinson and John Burnside. He has published four volumes of his own poetry. His latest book is *Perros en la playa* (Dogs on the Beach, 2011), a miscellany of poems, aphorisms and short essays. He currently lives in Madrid.

Sasha Dugdale is the author of three poetry collections, the most recent of which is *Red House*, published by Carcanet / Oxford Poets in 2012. She is a translator of poetry and plays and her translations of Russian poets are published by Bloodaxe. Her translation of the Russian poet Elena Shvarts *Birdsong on the Seabed* (Bloodaxe) was a PBS Recommended Translation and shortlisted for the Popescu and Academica Rossica prizes. She is Editor of *Modern Poetry in Translation*.

Nausheen Eusuf is a doctoral student in English at Boston University. She holds an MA in creative writing from Johns Hopkins, and her work has appeared in *Acumen*, *Orbis*, *The Interpreter's House*, *Poetry Salzburg Review*, and other journals. Her chapbook *What Remains* was recently published by Longleaf Press at Methodist University.

Adam Feinstein is a writer, journalist, poet and translator. His biography, *Pablo Neruda: A Passion for Life,* was published by Bloomsbury in 2004 to worldwide acclaim from, among others, Harold Pinter and Andrew Motion. He has translated from the work of many Spanish and Latin American poets, including Federico García Lorca and Mario Benedetti. He writes on Spanish and Latin American cultural and political affairs, as well as autism, for many publications around the world and also broadcasts on these subjects for the BBC. His latest book - his translations from Neruda's *Canto General*, illustrated with original prints by the Brazilian artist, Ana Maria Pacheco - will be published in 2013. He is currently working on a collection of translations from the Spanish poet, Félix Grande, and a book about cultural policy in Cuba since the Revolution.

Sally Festing's second chapbook is *Salaams* (Happenstance, 2009). She runs Saltmarsh Poetry in North Norfolk's Burnhams, and her sixth prose volume, *Showmen: the Voice of Travelling Fair People*, (Sean Tyas) is out this year.

Mary Fitzpatrick holds writing degrees from University of California Santa Cruz and University of Massachusetts Amherst, and works as a communications manager in a large corporation. Her poems have been featured in *Mississippi Review, Atlanta Review* and *North American Review* as contest finalists; and have been published in *Agenda, The Dos Passos Review, ASKEW, The Georgetown Review*, on-line by *Writers at Work* (L.A.), and in the 2011 anthology *A Bird Black as the Sun* (Green Poet Press).

Grey Gowrie's *Third Day: New and Selected Poems* (2008) was a Poetry Book Society Recommendation and a Book of the Year in *The Guardian* and the *Observer*. A new collection, *The Italian Visitor* is published by Carcanet this Spring. Born in Dublin in 1939, he was educated and professionally engaged in England and the USA, but made his home in Ireland until 1983. He now lives in the Welsh Marches. He has been Minister for the Arts, Chairman of the Art Council of England and Provost (i.e. Chancellor) of The Royal College of Art.

John Griffin was born in Tipperary, Ireland. He attended St. Louis University and Washington University (USA), where he read for his PhD. He currently lives and works in Riyadh, Saudi Arabia. His work has been published in many journals and first book of poems, *After Love*, came out earlier this year.

Harry Guest, poet, novelist and translator lives in Exeter. He edited and translated Penguin's *Post-war Japanese Poetry* in 1972. Many of his works have been published and his latest collection, *Some Times*, was brought out by Anvil Press in 2011.

Melisa Gürpınar was born in Istanbul in 1941. She studied drama in the Istanbul State Conservatory, then in London during the 60's in the broadcasting section of the BBC World Service. A prolific poet, she has won several awards and has been a prominent member of Turkish P.E.N.. Her poetry is characterized by a fine sensibility tempered by a strong sense of place and history, (mistaken sometimes for 'nostalgia') and rescued from melancholy by startling imagery and a gentle wit.

Gëzim Hajdari was born in 1957 in Hajdaraj, Albania, from a family of land owners whose property was confiscated during the dictatorship of Enver Hoxha. Because of his outspoken opposition to the regime & the post-Communist government, he was forced to leave Albania in 1992 following repeated threats. Since 1993 Hajdari, who writes both in Albanian and Italian, has published twelve collections of poetry (among which are *Corpo presente/ Trup i pranishëm, Stigmate/ Vragë, Spine Nere/ Gjëmba të zinj, Maldiluna/Dhimbjehëne, Poema dell'esilio / Poema e mërgimit*) & several other works including *Këngët e nizamit* (a collection of the songs of Albanian soldiers conscripted in the Ottoman army). For his literary merits, Hajdari has been nominated honorary citizen of Frosinone, the Italian town south of Rome where he has lived in exile since 1992.

Norbert Hirschhorn is a physician specializing in international public health, commended in 1993 by President Bill Clinton as an "American Health Hero." He now lives in London and Beirut. His poems have been published in over thirty journals, a dozen anthologies, four pamphlets, and three full collections: *A Cracked River,* Slow Dancer Press, London (1999); *Mourning in the Presence of a Corpse* (2008), and *Monastery of the Moon*, Dar al-Jadeed, Beirut (2012). His work has won a number of prizes in the US and UK.

177

The Cut of the Light: Poems 1965-2005 (Enitharmon) is a substantial selection from **Jeremy Hooker**'s ten volumes of poetry. His other books include *Welsh Journal* (Seren 2001) and *Writers in a Landscape* (University of Wales Press, 1996). His features for BBC Radio 3 include *A Map of David Jones* and *Daring the Depths*. He is an Emeritus Professor of the University of Glamorgan.

Rosalind Hudis has had poetry and fiction accepted for publication by a number of journals including *Stand*, the *Interpreter's House* and *The Lampeter Review*. In 2011 she won the Wilfred Owen Bursary and was short-listed for two Cinnamon Press competitions. One of her poems was awarded a commendation in the 2011 National Poetry Competition. She lives near Tregaron, West Wales and is studying for an MA in Creative Writing at trinity St David's, Lampeter.

Nigel Jarrett is a freelance writer and music critic based in Wales. He is a winner of the Rhys Davies Award for short fiction. In 2011 Parthian published *Funderland*, his debut collection of stories, which was universally praised in the national Press and elsewhere and longlisted for the Edge Hill Prize. His essays and poetry are published widely.

Ziba Karbassi was born in Tabriz, Iran in 1974 but had to leave her homeland in the mid-1980s and has since lived in exile in London. She has published eight books of poetry and is widely acknowledged as one of the very best and most influential of contemporary poets in Persian. Although banned in Iran, her work is much read there online and is particularly loved by younger generations. A chapbook in English translation *Collage Poems* was published by Exiled Writers Ink in 2009 and a trilingual (Persian, Italian and English) book with CD came out from Mille Gru in Milan in 2011. A full collection in translation is due to be published, individual poems having previously appeared in such journals as *Poetry Review, Modern Poetry in Translation, Shearsman, The Wolf, Fire, Tears In The Fence* and in the USA.

Birhan Keskin was born in Turkey in 1963. She graduated from Istanbul University in 1986 with a degree in sociology. Her first poems began to appear in 1984. From 1995 to 1998 she was joint editor of a small magazine and then worked as editor for a number of prominent publishing houses in Istanbul. Between 1991 and 2002 five books of her poetry were published by Metis. In 2005 she won the important Golden Orange award for her collection, *Ba*. In 2010 *Cold Dig* was published, from which these translations come.

Melinda Lovell lives, gardens, walks and writes in the foothills of the Cantal, South West France. She has had poems published or forthcoming in a variety of magazines including *The Rialto, The Frogmore Papers, Tears In The Fence, Pennine Platform, The Journal, Agenda, Other Poetry, The SHOp. The North*. She was short-listed for the Frogmore Poetry Prize in 2008 and 2010. She also runs a chapbook enterprise called Inchivala Press with her younger daughter.

Richard McKane, poet and translator from the Russian of Anna Akhmatova (Penguin, OUP and Bloodaxe), Olga Sedakova (Approach Books) and Larissa Miller (Arc). Anvil Press and Rockingham Press have also published his work, co-translated at times with Ruth Christie. He has also been an interpreter for Torture victims.

Merryn McCarthy taught for many years and moved from the countryside in England to the Gers region of South West France a few years ago. She has had poems published in several journals, including *English* and *Agenda*. Her collection, *Playing Truant*, is published by *Agenda* Editions.

Stuart Medland has written two collections of poems for children. Much of his writing is inspired by natural history and a forthcoming book, *Rings in the Shingle*, published by Brambleby Books, is a poetic celebration of Norfolk wildlife inspired by his own photographic encounters. *Ouzel on the Honister,* a collection of poems taken from his many visits to the Lake District over the years, is in preparation with Original Plus.

W.S. Milne is a regular contributor to *Agenda*. He has recently reviewed Samuel Beckett's *Collected Letters* in *PNR*. He is currently engaged on a prose translation in Scots of the *Iliad*.

Deborah Moffatt was born in Vermont and lives in Fife. Her poems have been widely published in the UK and Ireland. Her first collection of poetry, *Far From Home*, was published by Lapwing (Belfast) in 2004. She recently won the Baker Prize 2012 and was also included in *Poems of the Decade; an anthology of the Forward books of poetry 2002-2011*.

Pablo Neruda, the Chilean poet who won the Nobel Prize for Literature in 1971, was called 'the greatest poet of the twentieth century in any language' by Gabriel García Márquez. Neruda's reputation was made by his 1924 collection, *Twenty Love Poems and a Song of Despair*. After witnessing at first hand the horrors of the Spanish Civil War, including the murder of his great friend, Federico García Lorca, in August 1936, his poetry underwent a key metamorphosis – from one of self-obsessed anguish to a weapon for social and political justice. The immense richness of his poetry ranges from the hermetic beauty of *Residence on Earth* and the epic lyricism of *Canto General* to the crystalline joy of the *Elementary Odes* and the magnificent self-deprecating humour of *Extravagaria*. Neruda died on September 23, 1973, twelve days after the bloody military coup led by General Augusto Pinochet. In February 2013, a Chilean judge ordered the exhumation of Neruda's body to investigate the possibility that he might have been poisoned.

Alex Niven is writing a D.Phil on Basil Bunting at St John's College, Oxford. He has published on James Joyce and has an article forthcoming in *English Literary History* on Bunting's post-war trajectory. Originally from Hexham in Northumberland, his first book *Folk Opposition* was published in 2011. He is currently working on two book projects and his first collection of poems.

Ruth O'Callaghan is a nominee for the Pushcart Prize, a Hawthornden Fellow, competition adjudicator, interviewer, reviewer editor, workshop leader and mentor. Translated into six languages, she has read extensively in Asia, Europe and the USA where her audiences ranged, as the only poet, her audiences ranged from approximately one thousand to those on a buffalo farm and a ukulele players' convention. She has also recently completed a successful TV/Reading tour in New York and Boston. In 2009, the Arts Council sponsored her to visit Mongolia to collaborate with women poets on a book and a C.D. In the same year she was invited to the XXIX World Congress of Poets in Budapest and in 2010 to she was awarded a gold medal in Taiwan for her poetry. She was also awarded a Heinrich Böll residency in Eire in 2010 and is the poet for *Strandlines*, a community, multi-disciplinary project run under the auspices of Kings College, University of London. She is also working on a book of interviews with internationally renowned women poets and her new collection of poetry *The Silence Unheard* is due out early in 2013.

Francis O'Gorman is a Professor of English at the University of Leeds.

Liam O'Muírthile is from Cork, Ireland. His latest collection, *An Fuíoll Feá – Wood Cutting – New & Selected Poems*, was published by Cois Life in February.

Jeremy Page has edited *The Frogmore Papers* since 1983. He is the author of several collections of poems, most recently *In and Out of the Dark Wood* (Happen*Stance*, 2010). His work has been translated into German and Romanian, and a selection of his poems was recently broadcast on Radio Romania Cultural in English and Romanian. His own translations of Catullus are published by Ashley Press as *The Cost of All Desire*. He teaches at the University of Sussex.

Alexandra Petrova was born in Russia, spent some time in Jerusalem, and now lives outside Rome where she occasionally guides Russian tourists. She is an award-winning poet with three collections to her name, the latest of which is *Just the Trees*, published in 2008. She is currently writing a novel.

Sheenagh Pugh lived for many years in Cardiff, teaching creative writing at the University of Gamorgan, but now lives in Shetland. Her current collection is *Long-Haul Travellers* (Seren 2008) and another, *Short Days, Long Shadows*, is due out from Seren in 2014.

Omar Sabbagh is a widely published poet and critic. His poetry and prose has appeared or is forthcoming in venues such as: *Poetry Review, The Reader, The Warwick Review, PN Review, Poetry Wales, Wasafiri, The Wolf, Kenyon Review, Stand, Poem, The London Magazine, Banipal,* and elsewhere. His three extant poetry collections are: *My Only Ever Oedipal Complaint* and *The Square Root of Beirut* (Cinnamon Press, 2010, 2012); and *Waxed Mahogany* (Agenda Editions, 2012). For the years 2011-13 he is Visiting Assistant Professor in English Literature and Creative Writing at the American University of Beirut (AUB).

Adnan al-Sayegh was born in al-Kufa, Iraq in 1955. Conscripted into the army at the time of the Iraq-Iran war, he later fell foul of Saddam Hussein's regime and had to flee his country. Sayegh's is a poetry of migration and displacement : a nomadic record documented by the dates and place-names he tags many of his poems with. He has published ten books in Arabic including the 500-plus page epic *Uruk's Anthem* and he has a chapbook in English translation *The Deleted Part* (Exiled Writers Ink, 2009). His long poem in 16 parts *Pages From The Biography Of An Exile* was published in translation in *Long Poem Magazine* and a full-length bilingual collection by the present translators is with a UK publisher. He has lived in London since 2004, having previously spent a number of years in Sweden and in various other cities.

Daniele Serafini, born in 1952, graduated from Bologna University in 1980. His poetry collections are *Paesaggio celtico* (1993) which was a finalist for the Diego Valeri Prize; *Luce di confine* (1994); *Eterno chiama il mare* (1997) which gained an honourable mention at the Eugenio Montale International Prize; and *Dopo l'amore* (2004). His short novel *Café Hàwelka* also appeared in 1995 from Mobydick, Faenza which has published all his work. He is Head of the Museum Services in Lugo near Ravenna and Curator of the Francesco Baracca Museum of Aviation. He has edited the poetry-magazines *Origini* and *Tratti* and translated many poems from French and English. His own work has been translated into several European languages.

Sudeep Sen's *Fractals: New & Selected Poems/Translations: 1979-2013* was launched by Derek Walcott at the Nobel Laureate Week in St Lucia. His many books include: *Postmarked India* (HarperCollins), *Aria* (A K Ramanujan Translation Award), *Blue Nude* (Jorge Zalamea International Poetry Prize), and *The HarperCollins Book of English Poetry* (as editor). Recently, he won the Poetry Society Stanza Runners-Up Prize for his poem 'Banyan Stripes'; and 'Choice' that appeared in *Prairie Schooner* has been nominated for a Pushcart Prize. His works have appeared in *the TLS, Guardian, Newsweek, FT, BBC,* and others. He edits *Atlas*.

Robert Smith is a Londoner who now lives in Cambridge. His poetry is strongly influenced by music, and makes vivid use of imagery for its effects. He has been published previously in Agenda.

Gerard Smyth was born in Dublin where he still lives. His seventh collection, *The Fullness of Time: New and Selected Poems* (Dedalus Press, Dublin) was published in 2010 and appeared in an Italian translation this year. He was the 2012 recipient of the O'Shaughnessy Poetry Award from the University of St Thomas in Minnesota. He is a member of Aosdána and Poetry Editor of *The Irish Times*.

A.N. Stencl (1897-1983) was born in Czeladz in Poland. In his early twenties he moved to Berlin and was active in Yiddish & bohemian literary circles in the Weimar Republic, writing memorable poetry. In 1936 he managed to flee Germany and settled in Whitechapel in London's East End. There he edited for almost fifty years the journal *Loshn un lebn* and became a sort of indispensable walking archive of Yiddish emigrant culture. A bilingual edition of his Berlin-period poetry was published by Five Leaves (Nottingham) in 2007 with translations by Khayke Beruriah Wiegand and Stephen Watts. The present translations in *Agenda* are all from his London years.

Maria Taylor is a poet and reviewer from Leicestershire. She has had poetry published in a variety of magazines including *The North, Staple, The Guardian Online* and *Iota*. She has also reviewed for *The TLS* and *Sphinx*. Her debut collection, *Melanchrini*, is available from Nine Arches Press in July 2012.

Marek Urbanowicz has been published in a number of magazines such as *Agenda*, *Frogmore Papers*, *South*, *Weyfarers*. A former chairman of Brighton Poets, he started writing poetry at fourteen and never stopped. He has been a qualified acupuncturist since 1979.

Cristina Viti's published translations include *Selected Works of Dino Campana* (Survivors' Press 2006), Stephen Watts's *Mountain Language/Lingua di montagna*, *Journey Across Breath/Tragitto nel respiro* (Hearing Eye 2008, 2011) and *Gramsci & Caruso* (forthcoming for Mille Gru), Ziba Karbassi's *Poesie* (Mille Gru 2010), Dome Bulfaro's *Ossa Carne* (Le voci della luna 2012). Other translations (Elsa Morante, Amelia Rosselli, Eros Alesi, Erri De Luca, Ubax Ali Farah, Tahar Lamri) and/or own poetry have been published in *MPT, Shearsman Magazine, Wasafiri, L'Immaginazione, Scarf Magazine, VLAK*. Forthcoming translations include Mariapia Veladiano's award-winning novel *La vita accanto* (*A Life Apart*, MacLehose Press 2013) and a new version of Dino Campana's *Orphic Songs* (Waterloo Press 2014).

Stephen Watts is a poet, editor and translator. Among his own most recent books are *Mountain Language/Lingua di montagna* (2008) and *Journey Across Breath/Tragitto nel respire* (2011), both published by Hearing Eye and with Italian translation by Cristina Viti. *Ancient Sunlight* is forthcoming from Enitharmon in autumn 2013 and *The Language Of It* is due from Shearsman. His co-translations include chapbooks by Ziba Karbassi and Adnan al-Sayegh, *All My Young Years* by A.N. Stencl, *Ljubljana* by Meta Kušar and anthologies of Slovenian & Kurdish poetry. He edited Amarjit Chandan's *Sonata For Four Hands* for Arc in 2010 and is currently working on translations of Tonino Guerra, Victor Sunyol. He has completed full length collections of Ziba Karbassi and Adnan al-Sayegh. He has been poet in residence in many schools and hospitals, and he researches issues of language, creativity, well-being and migration.

Colin Wilcockson, retired Professor of Pembroke College, Cambridge. Medieval scholar, and trustee for *Agenda* over the last decade.

Stephen Yeo has had poems published in *Poetry Review, The Interpreters House, Friends Quarterly, Oxford Magazine, Isis* and in an earlier, online edition of *Agenda*. The poem in this 'Exiles' issue of *Agenda* was a runner-up in the *Keats-Shelley* prize a few years ago, and is part of a 'Chinese' sequence he is still working on. By trade he is a social historian and was formerly Principal of Ruskin College in Oxford.

www.agendapoetry.co.uk

**Visit Agenda's website for news, supplements of poems
and paintings, Broadsheets for young poets and artists,
reviews and essays.**

Subscribe online if you wish, and browse Agenda's online
bookshop.

Contents in online web supplement to the Exiles issue of Agenda:

POEMS AND PAINTINGS

REVIEWS:

Tim Liardet on Fiona Sampson's prose book: *Beyond the Lyric:
A Map of Contemporary British Poetry* (Chatto and Windus,
2012)

Omar Sabbagh on Sudeep Sen's *The Harper Collins Book of
English Poetry*

(Indian poets writing in English)

A list compiled by **Patricia McCarthy** of recommended poetry
collections

Special audio Exiles feature:
Eamon Grennan's dramatic production
of his long poem, 'Emigration Road'

TEAR–OFF SUBSCRIPTION FORM

Pay by cheque (payable to 'Agenda'), or
Visa / MasterCard

SUBSCRIPTION RATES ON INSIDE FRONT COVER

1 Subscription (1 year) =

2 double issues 1 double, 2 single issues or 4 single issues (The above is variable)

Please print

Name: ....

Address: ....

....

....

.... Postcode ....

Tel: ....

Email: ....

Visa / MasterCard No: ☐☐☐☐ – ☐☐☐☐ – ☐☐☐☐ – ☐☐☐☐

Expiry date: ☐☐ – ☐☐

Please tick box:

New Subscription ☐   Renewed Subscription ☐

(or subscribe online – www.agendapoetry.co.uk)

Send to: AGENDA, The Wheelwrights, Fletching Street, Mayfield,
East Sussex, TN20 6TL
Tel: 01435-873703